THE PROMETHEUS BOUND

OF

AESCHYLUS.

THE PROMETHEUS BOUND

OF

AESCHYLUS

EDITED BY

H. RACKHAM, M.A.

CAMBRIDGE
AT THE UNIVERSITY PRESS
1957

CAMBRIDGE UNIVERSITY PRESS
Cambridge, New York, Melbourne, Madrid, Cape Town,
Singapore, São Paulo, Delhi, Mexico City

Cambridge University Press
The Edinburgh Building, Cambridge CB2 8RU, UK

Published in the United States of America by Cambridge University Press, New York

www.cambridge.org
Information on this title: www.cambridge.org/9781107619975

First edition 1899
First published 1899
Reprinted 1903, 1927, 1940, 1957
First paperback edition 2013

A catalogue record for this publication is available from the British Library

ISBN 978-1-107-61997-5 Paperback

CONTENTS.

PREFACE.

THIS edition was undertaken at the suggestion of the Syndics of the University Press, and is intended to conform with the general plan of the Series in which it appears.

In preparing it I have drawn largely on the stores of material for the study of Aeschylus collected by Wecklein. The extent of my indebtedness to his textual edition (Berlin, 1885) is indicated at the beginning of the Critical Notes; while the Introduction and Explanatory Notes owe much to his commentaries in German (Leipzig, 1893) and in Greek (Athens, 1896). Among other editions of Aeschylus from which I have derived assistance, I must mention Dindorf's, Hermann's and Paley's; among translations, those of Mrs Browning and Miss Swanwick. Shortly before going to press I had the advantage of consulting a new edition of the *Prometheus* by Messrs Sikes and Willson, who have made a fresh collation of the Medicean MS., correcting that of Vitelli in one or two passages : my debts to these editors are acknowledged in several of the Critical Notes. So also are my obligations to Mr Walter G. Headlam, of King's College, who has kindly communicated to me some unpublished suggestions* to supplement his notes in the *Journal of Philology* and the *Classical Review.*

I have commented somewhat fully on grammatical points, adding references throughout to the sections of Goodwin's *Greek Grammar* (London, 1895), which I have denoted by G.

My thanks are due to my friend Mr E. Seymer Thompson, of Christ's College, for his kindness in reading through the Notes in proof.

H. R.

CHRIST'S COLLEGE, CAMBRIDGE,
    July, 1899.

I have made a few corrections in the text and notes of this edition on its being reprinted for the second time.

H. R.

    October, 1926.

---

* Since published in the *Classical Review*, XIV. p. 106 and *J. Phil.* XXX. p. 291 (where at l. 118 Headlam would read τερμόνιον ἐπὶ πάγον πόνων ἐμῶν θεωρὸς ἵκετ', ἢ ...).

INTRODUCTION.

The Prometheus Myth and Attic Ritual.

THERE is a tendency among primitive races to assign the discovery of the arts of life to some mythical individual, a personification of the inventive spirit of man. Such a 'culture-hero' among the ancient Greeks was Prometheus.

His chief title to fame was as the bringer of fire to men. As a fire-god he was worshipped at Athens in close connexion with Athena and Hephaestus. Prometheus and Hephaestus had a common altar in the suburb of the Academy, which was especially sacred to Athena. This altar was the starting-point of the torch-race that formed part of the annual festival in honour of Prometheus, as also of the Hephaestean and Pana-thenaic festivals. Lighting their torches at this altar, the racers ran to an altar in the city, the winner being he who reached it first with his torch alight and kindled a fire upon it.

Such torch-races were not uncommon. The ceremony is explained[1] as originating in a belief that fire becomes polluted by use or accident, and must from time to time be renewed. A new and pure fire would be kindled on some special altar, and thence conveyed to the other altars or hearths of the people where the old fires had been extinguished in readiness. To preserve its purity the new fire would be carried as rapidly as

[1] Wecklein in *Hermes* VII. p. 437; also Frazer's *Pausanias* II. p. 392.

possible, either by a single runner or (if the distance were great) by relays of runners who passed it on from hand to hand. This custom would easily develop into a race between competing runners, or as was sometimes the case between teams of runners.

The use of fire being one of the first elements of civilization, Prometheus, like Athena and Hephaestus, was associated with the arts and crafts, many of which he first taught to man ; and like Athena he was regarded as specially gifted with wisdom and foresight, as his name implied[1].

Various popular stories clustered round his name. He originally made men out of clay[2] (the remains of which were to be seen near Panopeus in Phocis[3]), and equipped them with attributes obtained from different animals[4]. When Zeus swallowed his wife, Prometheus[5] broke open his head to let out Athena. He stole fire from Zeus and conveyed it to men in a fennel-stalk[6]; and was punished by Zeus by being chained

---

[1] The connexion of Προμηθεύς with Skt. *pramantha*, the fire-stick used by savages for kindling fire by friction with another piece of wood, is now generally abandoned (Gardner and Jevons, *Manual of Greek Antiquities*, p. 79). Whatever its origin, the name was certainly associated in the Greek mind with προμήθεια : cf. P. V. 86, and the contrasted Ἐπιμηθεύς, 'after-thought.'

[2] Apollod. 1. 7. 1, Ov. Met. 1. 82 ; cf. Anth. Pal. 6. 352, an epigram of Erinna on a life-like picture, λῶστε Προμαθεῦ, ἔντι καὶ ἄνθρωποι τὶν ὁμαλοὶ σοφίαν.

[3] Paus. 10. 4. 3.

[4] Hor. Od. 1. 16. 13. According to Plato Protag. c. xi, the gods modelled men and animals of clay, and commissioned Prometheus and Epimetheus to equip them. Epimetheus having used up all the available attributes for the animals, there was nothing left for men, till Prometheus stole for them τὴν ἔντεχνον σοφίαν σὺν πυρὶ from the workshop of Hephaestus and Athena.

[5] Or according to others [e.g. Pind. Ol. 7. 35] Hephaestus: Apollod. 1. 3. 6.

[6] Ignem ferulis optime seruari certum est, Plin. N. H. 13. 22. A fennel-stalk is still used in the Greek islands as a means of carrying a light (A. Lang in *Encycl. Brit.*, Art. *Prometheus*).

on a desolate mountain, whence he was at last released by
Heracles.

The connexion of the origin of fire with a theft is found in
the legends of many different lands. It has been suggested
that the idea arose from the difficulty of producing fire artificially
in primitive times. Every early community kept a common
fire constantly burning, from which a light could be obtained
when needed : this was the origin of the sacred fires in the
Prytanea of Greek cities and the Temple of Vesta at Rome.
Supposing the common fire were allowed to go out, the tribe
would have to borrow, or if at war, to steal fire from its neigh-
bours. 'Men accustomed to such a precarious condition might
readily believe that the first possessors of fire, whoever they
were, set a high value on it and refused to communicate it to
others. Hence the belief that fire was originally stolen[1].'

The Prometheus legends further embody the primitive idea
of the essential impiety of human progress[2]. Early man tended
to regard the established order as divinely ordained, and
innovation however useful as an offence against the gods.
Religion is notoriously conservative ; and the inventive and
progressive spirit is apt to be lacking in humility and reverence.
This aspect of Prometheus was brought into prominence when
the popular tales were woven into a connected story by the
poets.

Prometheus in Hesiod.

Hesiod tells the story as follows (Theog. 521): The wise
Prometheus was the son of the Titan Iapetus and the Ocean-
nymph Clymene, and had a foolish brother named Epimetheus.
Prometheus came to trouble by vying with Zeus in wisdom.
Once when there was a dispute between gods and men [about
their respective shares in sacrifices], Prometheus sacrificed an
ox, and set the flesh wrapped in the hide on one side and the
bones covered with fat on the other, inviting Zeus to choose his
share. Though aware of the trick [this looks like a pious

[1] A. Lang, *ibid.*
[2] Cf. Hor. Od. 1. 3. 27, Audax Iapeti genus..., and the context.

perversion of the story], Zeus chose the bones,—and hence ever since men have burnt only the bones of sacrifices,—but was angry and withheld fire from men. But the beneficent Prometheus stole it and gave it to them. Then Zeus bound him with chains, and sent his eagle to devour his liver all the day, while it was made whole again every night. At last however Zeus relented, and allowed Heracles to win glory by slaying the eagle and releasing Prometheus.—Meanwhile, to punish men, Zeus caused Hephaestus to model a woman out of clay and Athena to adorn her, and sent this καλὸν κακόν to plague them. The foolish Epimetheus accepted the gift, and ever since women have been the bane of men's lives.—So impossible it is to cheat the mind of Zeus.

The story is repeated in the *Works and Days* 47—105. Here the woman is endowed by all the gods, and called Pandora. Before her coming men had lived free from all evils, but she took the lid off the jar and let them go abroad among men; hope alone was left in the jar, as she clapped the lid on again before it could fly away.

Hesiod has blended myth with allegory and made it a vehicle for moralizing and for satire. His Prometheus has the characteristics of cunning, benevolence towards men, and antagonism to the gods. He presides over the sacrifice in virtue of being the god of fire: this part of the legend is a mythological explanation of the Greek ritual, in which the whole burnt-offering of primitive times had dwindled down into burning for the gods only the fat and bones of the victim, while the worshippers feasted on the meat[1]. It is curious that the story contains the modelling out of clay and equipping of a human being, but gives no part in this to Prometheus. The allegory of the jar of evils is an awkward addition to the original account, in which the woman herself is the evil with which men are punished. The meaning of the allegory is obscure: it is not apparent whether hope is a good or an ill, and whether it is denied to men or kept back for them.—Nothing perhaps shows

---

[1] Tylor, *Primitive Culture* II. p. 400.

more strikingly the poetic genius of Aeschylus than a comparison of the noble tragedy created by him from the Prometheus legend with this crude, archaic story in Hesiod.

Aeschylus : The Prometheus Trilogy.

The treatment of the legend by Aeschylus is not before us in its entirety. Besides the Προμηθεὺς Δεσμώτης, the catalogue of his plays in the Codex Mediceus includes a Προμηθεὺς Πυρφόρος and a Προμηθεὺς Λυόμενος. Of the former two lines, of the latter considerable fragments alone survive[1] ; there is however little doubt that the three plays formed a connected trilogy, presenting the Prometheus myth in three successive parts[2]. The *Prometheus Vinctus* contains the punishment of Prometheus. The fragments of the *Prometheus Solutus* show that its subject was his release by Heracles ; and its connexion with the former play is proved by references in the scholia[3]. The connexion of the *Pyrphoros* is a strong presumption, but its contents and its position in the trilogy are left to conjecture. The obvious suggestion that it stood first, and exhibited the theft of fire, breaks down on examination : for the events leading to Prometheus' punishment are told so fully in the *Prometheus Vinctus* that they can hardly have formed the plot of a preceding

[1] Aesch. frr. 190 ff. Weckl. (187 ff. Dind.).

[2] Aeschylus also wrote a satyric drama on the Prometheus legend : see frr. 205—7 Weckl. (189, 190, 195 Dind.). (i) The hypothesis of the Persae states that he was victorious with the Phineus, Persae, Glaucus and Prometheus. (ii) Pollux twice mentions a Προμηθεὺς πυρκαεύς of Aeschylus, quoting a line λινᾶ τε πίσσα κὠμολίνου μακροὶ τόνοι, where the anapaest in the 4th foot proves the play was not a tragedy.—Perhaps this satyric drama was entitled simply Προμηθεύς, πυρκαεύς being added by the Alexandrian grammarians to distinguish it from the Prometheus trilogy produced later.

[3] Ad P. V. 527, οὔπω μοι λυθῆναι μεμοίραται· ἐν γὰρ τῷ ἐξῆς δράματι λύεται: ad 538 τῷ ἑξῆς δράματι φυλάττει τοὺς λόγους, 'the poet keeps the narrative for the following play.'

drama. We are forced to suppose that it concluded the trilogy[1].
It may have represented the institution of the worship of
Prometheus at Athens ; reasons for this conjecture will appear
when we have sketched the outline of the other two plays.

According to Aeschylus, Prometheus was the son of the pro-

P. Vinctus.   phetic goddess Themis. When Zeus made war
upon Cronus, Themis warned Prometheus that
craft and not force should gain the day : so since the Titans
rejected his counsels, he went over to the side of Zeus, who by
his aid defeated Cronus. Established on the throne, Zeus
allotted the gods their various offices, and then proposed to
destroy the human race and create a fresh one in its stead.
Prometheus opposed the design, and saved mankind, raising
them out of savagery by giving them fire and by teaching them
the arts of civilization, although he knew he would suffer for
thwarting Zeus's will. As a punishment, Zeus sent him in the
custody of his henchmen, Power and Might, to a lonely moun-
tain-gorge in Scythia [here the play begins], where Hephaestus
reluctantly fetters him to the rock. Left alone, Prometheus is
visited by the Ocean-nymphs, who vainly urge him to submission, and by Oceanus, whose offers of intercession with Zeus
he rejects with contempt. The frenzied Io comes wandering to
the spot. Her story is another instance of Zeus's tyranny, and
kindles Prometheus' wrath afresh. He imparts to her a secret
learnt from Themis, that Zeus will cause his own downfall by
marrying a woman destined to bear a son stronger than his
father : this danger Prometheus will only reveal at the price of
his own release, which shall be wrought by a descendant of Io.
Hermes next appears, sent by Zeus to demand the meaning of
the threatened danger. Prometheus refusing to disclose it,
Hermes warns him of the penalty for his contumacy : the earth
should be cleft, and the rock with Prometheus upon it be
engulfed ; after a long imprisonment beneath the ground he

---

[1] Schol. ad P. V. 94, ἐν γὰρ τῷ Πυρφόρῳ τρεῖς μυριάδας φησὶ δεδέσθαι
αὐτόν, seems to show that in the *Pyrphoros* the punishment of Prometheus
was over.

should rise again to the light, still hanging in chains, and the eagle of Zeus should be sent to prey upon his vitals : nor should this torture cease, until a god should take his sufferings on himself and descend into Hades in his stead. Prometheus defies Zeus to do his worst, and his doom comes upon him. A storm breaks over him, and he sinks below the ground, the Ocean-nymphs staying by him to share his fate.

The drama thus outlined obviously postulates a sequel to complete it. A plot is laid down but not worked out. It turns on the mysterious danger threatening Zeus and known to Prometheus alone. His punishment for stealing fire is only the starting-point : the catastrophe is the further penalty of his refusal to disclose the secret. This he will only do in return for his release : and it is abundantly indicated that this release is to form the dénoûment. The unconscious prophecies of others are confirmed by the hints and later by the declarations of Prometheus himself, to whom the future is revealed by Themis[1]. He cannot end his sufferings by death ; he can only be released with the consent of Zeus ; yet Prometheus will not yield, the reconciliation will be mutual; Zeus will relent when a god is found to suffer in Prometheus' stead, and then Prometheus will be set free by Heracles[2].

How were these threads taken up in the remainder of the trilogy ?

The fragments of the *Prometheus Solutus* show that at the opening of the play Prometheus had returned to light again and was hanging in chains on the mountain as before, but now tortured by the eagle. To him enter the Chorus of Titans [who have been released, together with Cronus, by Zeus and lodged in the Elysian plains]; they have come from the Red Sea and Aethiopia, across the Phasis into Europe, to comfort Prometheus. He recounts to them his sufferings, and his longing for death which is denied him ; and he recapitulates his services to man. Heracles arrives, and invoking Apollo's aid shoots the eagle

P. Solutus.

[1] 27, 525; 180, 206, 274, 529, 779, 898, 939; 101 n.
[2] 779, 965; 274; 206, 1023, 1034; 1058, 898.

and liberates Prometheus.   Prometheus foretells to Heracles his wanderings and labours.

Further circumstances agreeing with the hints of the *Prometheus Vinctus* can be derived from the references of later writers. The reconciliation foretold ⟍was brought about : Prometheus disclosed the secret, and Heracles was sent by Zeus to release him[1]. The substitute was found in Chiron the centaur ; accidentally shot by Heracles, he longed for death to relieve his incurable wound, but being immortal could not die, till he was offered to Zeus as an atonement for Prometheus[2]. The liberated Prometheus assumed a wreath of withes[3] as a memorial of his bonds.

How the reconciliation was brought about we do not know. Wecklein plausibly conjectures that the mediator was Ge, who is named with Heracles among the *dramatis personae* of the *Prometheus Vinctus* in the Medicean MS., and may have belonged like Heracles to the *Solutus.*

The Myth in Aeschylus.

We notice here several fresh elements in the story. (i) The plan of Zeus to destroy mankind is not in Hesiod, though there Zeus is no friend to man : κακὰ δ' ὄσσετο θυμῷ θνητοῖς ἀν-θρώποισι, Theog. 551. It is a primitive legend paralleled in the mythologies of other lands. (ii) Prometheus is now the son of Themis, no father being mentioned. Themis was identified

225 n. with Ge in Attic worship ; so that this may have been the version of his parentage accepted at Athens: it serves the poet to account for his prophetic powers. (iii) The story of the danger of marriage with Thetis appears in another form in Pindar[4]: there her hand is desired by Poseidon as well as

---

[1] Hygin. fab. 54, obviously from Aeschylus, v. Wecklein's Aeschylus (1896), II. p. 36.

[2] Apollod. 2. 5. 4 and 11.

[3] λύγου στέφανος, Athen. 672 E, 674 D: cf. fr. 202 Weckl. (204 Dind.). Withes were used as bonds, Athen. 671 F.

[4] Isthm. 7. 27 ff.

Zeus ; Themis warns the suitors of the oracle that Thetis shall bear a son stronger than his sire ; they relinquish her to Peleus, and the prophecy is fulfilled in Achilles. The adaptation of this legend to the story of Prometheus may be due to Aeschylus himself, whose version seems to be indebted to that of Pindar[1]. (iv) Chiron's vicarious atonement is remarkable. It formed an integral part of the plot, but how precisely it was worked in is not easy to see : since the disclosure of the secret by Prometheus would appear sufficient in itself to make Zeus relent.

The rebellion and reconciliation of Prometheus are treated by Aeschylus as part of the great myth of the revolution in heaven, the overthrow of Cronus and the Titans and the establishment of the new dynasty of Zeus and the gods who hold their offices from him. Stress is laid throughout the *Prometheus Vinctus* on the novelty of Zeus's rule : his cruelty to Prometheus is but a part of the insolence of the usurper towards the older gods[2]. So in the *Solutus* Prometheus is associated with the Titans in his recon-ciliation to the new order. In the Titanomachia we are pro-bably to see a mythological embodiment of a struggle between an old religion and a new. The Titans represent the supreme deities of an aboriginal race, ousted by the Olympian hierarchy of the Hellenic invaders, but still lingering on in popular imagination. Prometheus in the legends was the foe of Zeus ; Zeus was supreme in Attic worship, but Prometheus still re-tained his honours as the most ancient deity of fire. Aeschylus dramatizes a mythological explanation of the situation. If we accept the conjecture that the *Pyrphoros* presented the installa-tion of Prometheus at his altar in the Academy and the institution of the festival and torch-race in his honour, we have a close parallel in the Eumenides : there too Aeschylus has shown archaic deities 'overridden by the younger gods[3],' but finally reconciled to the new order and established in Attic worship as the guardians of retributive justice.

[1] Cf. note on 954 ff.—Prometheus appears at the marriage of Peleus and Thetis in Catullus 64. 294, so his connexion with that legend was well established.

[2] 35, 95, 156, 160, 175, 420.   [3] Eum. 734, 781 (731, 778).

Ethical meaning.

We are not however content to find in the Prometheus trilogy a mythological spectacle and nothing more. While constructing a dramatic presentation of legend and ritual, Aeschylus cannot but have had the further object of conveying some moral or religious teaching. Yet what exact teaching was intended, with only one of the three plays before us, is extremely hard to say. The question has been the subject of much controversy, the difficulty being to understand the poet's conception of Zeus. Elsewhere in Aeschylus Zeus is the embodiment not only of power but also of right. In the *Prometheus Vinctus* he seems to be shown as a tyrant and an oppressor : he cares nothing for men ; he cruelly persecutes their self-sacrificing benefactor, his former ally ; he abandons Io, the hapless victim of his passions, to unmerited suffering. What theory of morality or religion can be intended by such a picture ?

The view has been held that Aeschylus has here departed from his usual standpoint ; that he has accepted the darker side of the old legends as he found them, and for once has made Zeus the villain of the piece. For this reading of the play it is enough to refer to Shelley, who saw in Prometheus the personification of the human spirit, benevolent and progressive, indomitably struggling with the tyranny of superstition. But that this was not the conception of Aeschylus is shown by the fact that in his own *Prometheus Unbound* Shelley has felt compelled to depart from the Aeschylean myth : 'averse from a catastrophe so feeble as that of reconciling the Champion with the Oppressor of mankind[1],' he has supplied an ideal conclusion in which Jupiter is overthrown and Prometheus triumphs.

It is in fact impossible to credit Aeschylus with a conception so subversive, so at variance with his usual attitude of reverence towards the Hellenic religion. To do so is not merely to ignore the evidence for his development of the story in the later plays,

---

[1] Preface to Shelley's *Prometheus Unbound.*

but to overlook the hints to be gleaned from the *Prometheus Vinctus* itself. In this play the figure of Prometheus dominates the scene ; the story is presented entirely from his point of view. But there are still indications of another aspect in the background. The new ruler is charged by Prometheus and his friends with all the vices of autocracy[1]: he is arbitrary, cruel, and ungrateful. But these charges are not borne out by the facts. Zeus's accession was no lawless usurpation, but the replacement of the rule of force by the rule of wisdom. It was

228. fated that wisdom ('craft,' says Prometheus bitterly) should prevail over might ; nor was Zeus supported by Prometheus or Forethought only, but by Themis, the embodiment of Justice. The overthrow of Cronus fulfilled the will of Destiny ; Zeus

942. came under his father's curse, but the wrong was repaired by the release of Cronus : πέδας μὲν ἂν λύσειεν, ἔστι τοῦδ' ἄκος[2]. His harshness was shown only to his foes. The Titans opposed his sway and were punished, but had been forgiven before the opening of the *Prometheus Solutus*. Prometheus for all his former services only met with the punishment that his self-will

247 ff. deserved. He states that Zeus in his contempt for man would have destroyed the race and begotten another in its stead, had not he prevented this design by the gifts of hope, of fire, and of

458 ff. the arts, whereby he raised men from their former savagery. It would seem that the purpose of Zeus was but to let nature take its course, and allow the degraded race to perish of its own feebleness ; he intended then to replace it by another, created in his own image. If so, Prometheus' philanthropy was misguided : in saving the race he perpetuated human imperfection, and was justly punished for frustrating the divine wisdom. Even

30. his friend Hephaestus admits he was in error. Io again appears at first sight as the unhappy victim of a tyrant's caprice : but her sufferings, though arising from the love of Zeus, were directly

---

[1] 35, 158, 202, 237, 418. In spite of his own connexion with Hiero, Aeschylus under cover of dramatic requirements has given forcible expression to the hatred of tyrants that was so strongly felt by the Athenians.

[2] Eum. 648 (645).

617. caused by the jealousy of Hera.   Zeus's true purpose with her is
     confessed by the prophecy of Prometheus: restored to human
895 ff. form, she was to become the mother of a royal race, from which
     should spring the deliverer of Prometheus and the benefactor of
     mankind.   This aspect of her story was doubtless emphasized in
     the *Prometheus Solutus*, as it is in the Supplices[1]:

> Zeus, lord of ceaseless ages, thine,
> Oh thine was that unharming might!
> The breathing of thy love divine
> Arrests at length her toilsome flight,
> And gently with the mournful tide
> Of modest tears, her woes subside.
> Then, as Fame truly tells, receiving there
> Thy germ divine, her blameless child she bare,

> From age to age supremely blest.
> Hence the whole world proclaims, this seed,
> Life teeming, springs in very deed
> From Zeus, for who but he the pest
> Could stay, devised by Hera's spite?

In the *Prometheus Solutus*, we know, the Titans have been
forgiven and released, and Prometheus, reconciled with Zeus,
confesses his moral defeat by donning the wreath of withes as a
memorial of his bondage.

   If something like this was the intention of the poet, the
moral of the whole trilogy is the short-sightedness of human
wisdom, misjudging the plans of omnipotence, 'the harmony of
569. Zeus' (as even in the *Prometheus Vinctus* the Chorus recog-
     nize), 'that mortal counsels shall never overpass'; rebellion,
     justified for a time to outward seeming, is proved in error at the
     last.

   It must however be admitted that this interpretation is
hardly at one with the first impression produced by the play
before us.   As we read it, we are carried away by the heroic
grandeur of Prometheus.   His benevolence, his self-sacrifice, his
indomitable courage, form a character that takes possession of

---

[1] Supp. 582 (574) ff., Miss Swanwick's Translation.

our sympathies : we are compelled to be on his side, and to regard Zeus as an unjust oppressor. Possibly the succeeding dramas, though correcting, would be powerless to obliterate this impression. Perhaps we must say that in throwing all his powers into this sublime creation, Aeschylus was betrayed into an inconsistency, and created a difficulty that he was unable to solve. The parallel of Milton has been well suggested. 'The republican poet, urged on by his dramatic sympathies and by his love of freedom and independence, has drawn the 'unconquerable will' of Satan, and his 'courage never to submit or yield,' with so much force and enthusiasm, as to disturb the ethical balance of his general scheme ; and there is some justification for Shelley's criticism, that Satan is the real hero of *Paradise Lost*[1].'

Characters and Structure.

The *Prometheus Vinctus* may be called a one-part play. The minor characters are subordinated to the central figure, which occupies the stage throughout, impressive in silence as in speech.

The warders CRATOS and BIA (of whom the former only is made to speak) appear in Hesiod (Theog. 385) as the constant attendants of Zeus. Aeschylus draws them as the brutal satellites of a tyrant, as hard of heart as they are ferocious of aspect.
42,78. They contrast with the good-natured HEPHAESTUS, who is
45. disgusted with the task that his craft imposes on him. In his
11 n. matter-of-fact way he sees that Prometheus is in the wrong, but
30. he is loth to punish a kinsman and fellow-craftsman. Yet as
39. the work must be done, he feels a workmanlike satisfaction in
60,63. doing it well.

The CHORUS of Ocean-nymphs is happily conceived to lighten the gloom of the play, their fairy-like forms contrasting with the gigantic figures of the male characters. Their part is treated as a study in feminine sympathy. Curiosity has pre-
139. vailed over modesty to bring them to the scene, and is largely

---

[1] Haigh, *Tragic Drama of the Greeks*, p. 112.

blended with their compassion for Prometheus and for Io.
Towards Prometheus they waver between pity for his cruel
punishment and horror at the wilfulness that brought it upon
275. him. Revolt has failed, and they counsel submission: piety
542 ff. and humility alone can lead to happiness. Yet compassion is
their strongest feeling, and they nobly refuse to desert Prometheus in his extremity.

312 n. The pompous OCEANUS lends a touch of comedy, like the
Watchman in the Agamemnon and the Nurse in the Choephori.
He is a foil to the unyielding pride of Prometheus: a time-
server, boasting his influence with the tyrant. His sympathy
is only half sincere, and when his proffered mediation is rejected,
he retires with alacrity.

The pathetic figure of Io speaks for itself: her frenzy, her
calm despair, her romantic story are alike drawn with unsur-
passed grace. She is connected with the plot through her
descendant Heracles, the destined deliverer of Prometheus.
Her unmerited sufferings serve to heighten the captive's indignation ; while the prophecy of her restoration by Zeus, revealing
the true meaning of his dealings with her, prepares the way for
some justification of his treatment of Prometheus. Much of the
episode however is frankly pictorial: the marvellous recital of
Io's wanderings would not be felt to be unduly discursive by an
audience that delighted in the travellers' tales of Herodotus and
the wonders of the distant lands just opening to the knowledge
of the Greeks[1].

HERMES is the complacent servant of the new ruler. The
976 ff. insolence of 'Zeus's lackey' is sobered by the rising fury of the

---

[1] For the Io myth see notes on ll. 581, 875: for her wanderings,
the footnote on p. 75.—Io is represented in the play as a cow-horned
maiden (613), perhaps because she could not appear on the stage
completely transformed into a cow. In the Supplices, where she does
not appear, she is generally spoken of as βοῦς, πόρτις, but at 577 (568)
as βοτὸν μιξόμβροτον, τὰν μὲν βοός, τὰν δ' αὖ γυναικός. In early art she
was figured as a cow, but in the 5th c. as a maid with cow's horns—
possibly owing to the influence of the stage (Roscher's *Lexikon*, s. v.
Io).

captive. He passes into a tone of admonition, and finally, despairing of such a madman, departs with a last warning to the Ocean-nymphs.

The early Greek drama, with its chorus and single actor, was necessarily lyric and epic in style: it consisted mainly of long choral odes and narrative speeches. The introduction of a second actor by Aeschylus permitted the growth of the dramatic element; with three interlocutors the story could be evolved in action and dialogue instead of being narrated and sung. This change has not proceeded very far in the Supplices, Persae and Septem. The *Prometheus*, though retaining something of the early manner, shows a great advance. The choral odes are small[1], and detached from the rest of the play[2]. The Chorus has little connexion with the plot, and is falling into the position of a spectator[3], though still more prominent and more individualized in character than with Sophocles and Euripides. The story is acted on the stage, though the action is arrested by long narratives instead of developing continuously as in the Oresteia.

The structure of the play is not elaborate. A kind of plot is furnished by Prometheus' secret, but the thread is twice introduced and dropped again aimlessly, before being finally taken up to lead to the catastrophe[4]. The episodes of Oceanus and Io each serve a dramatic object, but their introduction is naïvely 288. abrupt. Oceanus interrupts the narrative promised by Prometheus to the Chorus. Io's entry is quite casual and unexplained. 864 n. It is hard to see a reason for the order in which her wanderings are told. Elsewhere[5] abrupt transitions are noticeable. Small

[1] Lyrics : dialogue as 1 : 7, as against 1 : 2 in the three early plays, and 1 : 3 even in the Oresteia. The peculiar situation may partly account for this brevity of the lyrics: Prometheus never leaving the stage, his silence while the Chorus sings is felt to be undramatic: at 451 he is actually made to apologize for it.

[2] Prometheus' account of Atlas is followed by an unconnected ode on the same theme, 441 ff.

[3] Oceanus takes no notice of his daughters' presence.

[4] 183 ff., 530 ff., 782, 939.   [5] 363, 452, 939.

inconsistencies may be detected : Zeus already intends to marry
Thetis, yet cannot guess what Prometheus' threats refer to;
the Ocean-stream is near enough for the Oceanides to hear the
sound of the hammering, but Oceanus magnifies his kindness
by speaking of the length of his journey. It is however absurd
to demand realism from a drama professedly supernatural[1]: in
its primeval wonderland the limitations of time and space are
328. ignored. Zeus overhears Prometheus from his throne on high;
and knows the rejection of his final command as soon as it is
1114. uttered, for the storm bursts as Hermes quits the stage.

Scene[2].

The scene is laid on a desolate mountain in Scythia[3]. It is
in sight of the sea; and near to the coast, since Io comes along
the shore. The coast seems to be that of the earth-encircling
Ocean-stream, for the mountain is on the confines of the earth,
and within hearing of the caves of the Ocean-nymphs.

Aeschylus therefore vaguely conceived the place of Prometheus' punishment as in the extreme north of the world. It
is not specified by Hesiod. A later account, first found
in Apollonius Rhodius, placed it in the Caucasus. The
Caucasus is mentioned as the scene of the play by the Hypothesis, which is probably to be ascribed to Aristophanes of
Byzantium; this is however corrected by a footnote in the
Medicean MS.: ἰστέον ὅτι οὐ κατὰ τὸν κοινὸν λόγον ἐν Καυκάσῳ
φησὶ δεδέσθαι τὸν Προμηθέα, ἀλλὰ πρὸς τοῖς Εὐρωπαίοις τέρμασιν
τοῦ Ὠκεανοῦ, ὡς ἀπὸ τῶν πρὸς τὴν Ἰὼ λεγομένων ἔστι συμβαλεῖν—
a reference to l. 745, where Io is to reach the Caucasus after
a long journey. Also at l. 438 the Caucasus is referred to as
having people dwelling near it, whereas the scene of the play is

---

[1] Aristotle, *Poet.* 1456 a 2, quotes the *Prometheus* as an instance of
τὸ τερατῶδες.

[2] See Allen in the *American Journal of Philology* xiii; also Foss,
De Loco in quo Prometheus apud Aeschylum vinctus sit, Bonn 1862.

[3] 2, 20; 89, 1122; 594; 118; 136.

a desert. It is true that both Cicero (Tusc. 2. 23) and Strabo (4. 182) place the scene of the *Prometheus Solutus* in the Caucasus, but it is most unlikely to have been other than that of the *Prometheus Vinctus*. Probably both Cicero and Strabo, like the writer of the Hypothesis, were misled by the account current in their days. Cicero's translation from the *Solutus* (*ibid.*) contains the words *saxa Caucasi*, but this may represent merely πέτραι in the original[1].

Representation.

The early plays of Aeschylus required only two actors to perform them. A third actor was first employed by Sophocles, whose first play appeared in 468 B.C.; and the innovation was adopted by Aeschylus in the Oresteia. Whether he used a third actor in the *Prometheus* is uncertain. There are never more than two characters on the stage together except in the first scene, and there Prometheus remains silent till the others have departed. It was suggested by Welcker that the form of Prometheus was represented by a lay-figure, from behind which the actor spoke the part. If this were so, the protagonist would be able to double the parts of Hephaestus and Prometheus; Cratos, Oceanus, Io and Hermes being all sustained by the deuteragonist. Bia is a κωφὸν πρόσωπον, and would be played by a supernumerary.

Welcker's suggestion may be thought far-fetched[2], but there are several considerations in its favour. Prometheus never quits the stage throughout the play, and speaks nearly one-half of the entire number of lines: to support this onerous part while standing fastened to a rock, even if the arms were left loose enough to allow a certain amount of action, would tax an actor's endurance very severely. The long silence of Prometheus, impressive and dramatic as it is, may well have been suggested by necessity. Elsewhere the play is constructed for two actors only. At l. 81 Hephaestus exits before Cratos, so that the

[1] Allen, *ibid.*

[2] Haigh rejects it as very improbable, *Attic Theatre*, edn. 2, p. 251.

protagonist would be able to take his place behind the lay-figure before l. 88. Between the scenes of Cratos, Oceanus, Io and Hermes are intervals filled by Prometheus and the Chorus, giving the deuteragonist time to rest and change his dress. If a lay-figure were employed, it may have been discovered in position at the beginning of the play, or drawn on, as Wecklein supposes, by Cratos and Bia. L. 74 appears to imply that Prometheus is represented as a figure of gigantic stature, and that Cratos and Bia have climbed up the rock to fetter his arms. The business of the wedge at 64 could be more easily managed with a lay-figure. Little weight, however, attaches to the latter considerations in the absence of conclusive evidence to show how far realism was aimed at in the staging of the Aeschylean drama: perhaps we may infer that circumstances fully described by the poet were left to the imagination of the spectators[1].

This uncertainty precludes our discussing how, if at all, the car of the Oceanides and the flying-horse of Oceanus were actually represented. As for the storm with which the play concludes, we may well believe that the poet's description was not supplemented by any attempt at realistic presentation. A βροντεῖον or thunder-machine and a κεραυνοσκοπεῖον, 'lightning-tower,' are mentioned among stage-accessories by Pollux, but can hardly have been used in the primitive Attic theatre. The play evidently ends with the fulfilment of the threat of Zeus: the earth opens and swallows up the rock with Prometheus on it; the Chorus, as Hermes has warned them and they themselves have promised, remain and share his fate. Accepting Doerpfeld's well-known theory that in the early Attic theatre there was no stage but only the orchestra, we should be forced to suppose that this catastrophe was left entirely to the imagination: there being no curtain, actor and chorus must have tamely walked off, or if a lay-figure of Prometheus was used, it was left in position for the *Prometheus Solutus.* But it is hard to see why Aeschylus introduced the engulfing of Prometheus at all, if it could not be exhibited. On the contrary, it

[1] See Gardner and Jevons, *Greek Antiquities*, pp. 685 ff.

has been suggested[1] that he invented the incident as the only possible way of getting the fettered actor or figure off the stage. And now that the balance of archaeological opinion seems to favour the view that in the time of Aeschylus there was a wooden stage raised above the orchestra, in which a trap-door would be practicable, we may believe that Prometheus on his rock, with the Chorus grouped about him, did actually sink out of sight[2].

Date.

When the play was first produced we do not know. The allusion to the eruption of Etna fixes a superior limit at 479 B.C., or 5 or 6 years later if the passage be copied from Pindar's First Pythian, which celebrates a victory won in 474. We have the further evidence of dramatic style (see p. xxiii.), which would place the *Prometheus* later than the Supplices, Persae (472 B.C.), and Septem (467 B.C.), but earlier than the Oresteia (458 B.C.). Aeschylus died in 456.

383 ff.

367 n.

[1] Allen, *ibid.*

[2] Wilamowitz-Moellendorff, *Die Buehne des Aischylos*, in *Hermes* xxi.

ΑΙΣΧΥΛΟΥ

ΠΡΟΜΗΘΕΥΣ ΔΕΣΜΩΤΗΣ

ΤΑ ΤΟΥ ΔΡΑΜΑΤΟΣ ΠΡΟΣΩΠΑ

ΚΡΑΤΟΣ ΚΑΙ ΒΙΑ
ΗΦΑΙΣΤΟΣ
ΠΡΟΜΗΘΕΥΣ
ΧΟΡΟΣ ΩΚΕΑΝΙΔΩΝ
ΩΚΕΑΝΟΣ
ΙΩ ΙΝΑΧΟΥ
ΕΡΜΗΣ

ΥΠΟΘΕΣΙΣ

Προμηθέως ἐν Σκυθίᾳ δεδεμένου διὰ τὸ κεκλοφέναι τὸ πῦρ πυνθάνεται Ἰὼ πλανωμένη ὅτι κατ' Αἴγυπτον γενομένη ἐκ τῆς ἐπαφήσεως τοῦ Διὸς τέξεται τὸν Ἔπαφον. Ἑρμῆς δὲ παράγεται ἀπειλῶν αὐτῷ κεραυνωθήσεσθαι, ἐὰν μὴ εἴπῃ τὰ μέλλοντα ἔσεσθαι τῷ Διί. προέλεγε γὰρ ὁ Προμηθεὺς ὡς ἐξωσθήσεται ὁ Ζεὺς τῆς ἀρχῆς ὑπό τινος οἰκείου υἱοῦ. τέλος δὲ βροντῆς γενομένης ἀφανὴς ὁ Προμηθεὺς γίνεται.

Κεῖται δὲ ἡ μυθοποιία ἐν παρεκβάσει παρὰ Σοφοκλεῖ ἐν Κολχίσι, παρὰ δὲ Εὐριπίδῃ ὅλως οὐ κεῖται. ἡ μὲν σκηνὴ τοῦ δράματος ὑπόκειται ἐν Σκυθίᾳ ἐπὶ τὸ Καυκάσιον ὄρος· ὁ δὲ χορὸς συνέστηκεν ἐξ Ὠκεανίδων νυμφῶν. τὸ δὲ κεφάλαιον αὐτοῦ ἐστι Προμηθέως δέσις.

ΠΡΟΜΗΘΕΥΣ ΔΕΣΜΩΤΗΣ

The lines are numbered as in Wecklein's edition (1885), following the Medicean MS. Dindorf's numbers (quoted by Liddell and Scott) are added in brackets where they differ.

[*Scene: a mountain ravine near the Ocean.*

Πρόλογος. *Enter* CRATOS *and* BIA, *leading* PROMETHEUS *as a prisoner; with them* HEPHAESTUS, *who carries fetters and a smith's hammer.*]

ΚΡ. Χθονὸς μὲν εἰς τηλουρὸν ἥκομεν πέδον,
Σκύθην ἐς οἶμον, ἄβατον εἰς ἐρημίαν.
Ἥφαιστε, σοὶ δὲ χρὴ μέλειν ἐπιστολὰς
ἅς σοι πατὴρ ἐφεῖτο, τόνδε πρὸς πέτραις
ὑψηλοκρήμνοις τὸν λεωργὸν ὀχμάσαι   5
*ἀδαμαντίνων δεσμῶν ἐν ἀρρήκτοις πέδαις.
τὸ σὸν γὰρ ἄνθος, παντέχνου πυρὸς σέλας,
θνητοῖσι κλέψας ὤπασεν· τοιᾶσδέ τοι
ἁμαρτίας σφὲ δεῖ θεοῖς δοῦναι δίκην,
ὡς ἂν διδαχθῇ τὴν Διὸς τυραννίδα   10
στέργειν, φιλανθρώπου δὲ παύεσθαι τρόπου.
ΗΦ. Κράτος Βία τε, σφῷν μὲν ἐντολὴ Διὸς
ἔχει τέλος δὴ κοὐδὲν ἐμποδὼν ἔτι·
ἐγὼ δ᾽ ἄτολμός εἰμι συγγενῆ θεὸν
δῆσαι βίᾳ φάραγγι πρὸς δυσχειμέρῳ   15

4 ΑΙΣΧΥΛΟΥ

πάντως δ' ἀνάγκη τῶνδέ μοι τόλμαν σχεθεῖν·
ἐξωριάζειν γὰρ πατρὸς λόγους βαρύ.

[*To* PROMETHEUS]

τῆς ὀρθοβούλου Θέμιδος αἰπυμῆτα παῖ,
ἄκοντά σ' ἄκων δυσλύτοις χαλκεύμασιν
προσπασσαλεύσω τῷδ' ἀπανθρώπῳ πάγῳ,   20
ἵν' οὔτε φωνὴν οὔτε του μορφὴν βροτῶν
ὄψῃ, σταθευτὸς δ' ἡλίου φοίβῃ φλογὶ
χροιᾶς ἀμείψεις ἄνθος· ἀσμένῳ δέ σοι
ἡ ποικιλείμων νὺξ ἀποκρύψει φάος,
πάχνην θ' ἑῴαν ἥλιος σκεδᾷ πάλιν·   25
ἀεὶ δὲ τοῦ παρόντος ἀχθηδὼν κακοῦ
τρύσει σ'· ὁ λωφήσων γὰρ οὐ πέφυκέ πω.
τοιαῦτ' ἐπηύρου τοῦ φιλανθρώπου τρόπου.
θεὸς θεῶν γὰρ οὐχ ὑποπτήσσων χόλον
βροτοῖσι τιμὰς ὤπασας πέρα δίκης.   30
ἀνθ' ὧν ἀτερπῆ τήνδε φρουρήσεις πέτραν
ὀρθοστάδην ἄυπνος, οὐ κάμπτων γόνυ·
πολλοὺς δ' ὀδυρμοὺς καὶ γόους ἀνωφελεῖς
φθέγξῃ· Διὸς γὰρ δυσπαραίτητοι φρένες·
ἅπας δὲ τραχὺς ὅστις ἂν νέον κρατῇ.   35

ΚΡ. εἶεν, τί μέλλεις καὶ κατοικτίζῃ μάτην;
     τί τὸν θεοῖς ἔχθιστον οὐ στυγεῖς θεόν,
     ὅστις τὸ σὸν θνητοῖσι προύδωκεν γέρας;

ΗΦ. τὸ συγγενές τοι δεινὸν ἥ θ' ὁμιλία.

ΚΡ. σύμφημ'· ἀνηκουστεῖν δὲ τῶν πατρὸς λόγων   40
     οἷόν τε; πῶς οὐ τοῦτο δειμαίνεις πλέον;

ΗΦ. ἀεί γε δὴ νηλὴς σὺ καὶ θράσους πλέως.

ΚΡ. ἄκος γὰρ οὐδὲν τόνδε θρηνεῖσθαι· σὺ δὲ
     τὰ μηδὲν ὠφελοῦντα μὴ πόνει μάτην.

ΗΦ. ὦ πολλὰ μισηθεῖσα χειρωναξία.   45

ΚΡ. τί νιν στυγεῖς; πόνων γὰρ ὡς ἁπλῷ λόγῳ
τῶν νῦν παρόντων οὐδὲν αἰτία τέχνη.

ΗΦ. ἔμπας τις αὐτὴν ἄλλος ὤφελεν λαχεῖν.

ΚΡ. ἅπαντ' *ἐπαχθῆ πλὴν θεοῖσι κοιρανεῖν.
ἐλεύθερος γὰρ οὔτις ἐστὶ πλὴν Διός.   50

ΗΦ. [Showing fetters]
ἔγνωκα τοῖσδε, κοὐδὲν ἀντειπεῖν ἔχω.

ΚΡ. οὔκουν ἐπείξῃ τῷδε δεσμὰ περιβαλεῖν,
ὡς μή σ' ἐλινύοντα προσδερχθῇ πατήρ;

ΗΦ. καὶ δὴ πρόχειρα ψάλια δέρκεσθαι πάρα.

ΚΡ. *βαλών νιν ἀμφὶ χερσὶν ἐγκρατεῖ σθένει   55
ῥαιστῆρι θεῖνε, πασσάλευε πρὸς πέτραις.

[CRATOS and BIA hold PROMETHEUS while HEPHAESTUS
chains him to a rock.]

ΗΦ. περαίνεται δὴ κοὐ ματᾷ τοὔργον τόδε.

ΚΡ. ἄρασσε μᾶλλον, σφίγγε, μηδαμῇ χάλα.
δεινὸς γὰρ εὑρεῖν κἀξ ἀμηχάνων πόρον.

ΗΦ. ἄραρεν ἥδε γ' ὠλένη δυσεκλύτως.   60

ΚΡ. καὶ τήνδε νῦν πόρπασον ἀσφαλῶς, ἵνα
μάθῃ σοφιστὴς ὢν Διὸς νωθέστερος.

ΗΦ. πλὴν τοῦδ' ἂν οὐδεὶς ἐνδίκως μέμψαιτό μοι.

ΚΡ. ἀδαμαντίνου νῦν σφηνὸς αὐθάδη γνάθον
στέρνων διαμπὰξ πασσάλευ' ἐρρωμένως.   65

ΗΦ. αἰαῖ, Προμηθεῦ, σῶν ὑπὲρ στένω πόνων.

ΚΡ. σὺ δ' αὖ κατοκνεῖς τῶν Διός τ' ἐχθρῶν ὕπερ
στένεις; ὅπως μὴ σαυτὸν οἰκτιεῖς ποτέ.

ΗΦ. ὁρᾷς θέαμα δυσθέατον ὄμμασιν.

ΚΡ. ὁρῶ κυροῦντα τόνδε τῶν ἐπαξίων.   70
ἀλλ' ἀμφὶ πλευραῖς μασχαλιστῆρας βάλε.

ΗΦ. δρᾶν ταῦτ' ἀνάγκη, μηδὲν ἐγκέλευ' ἄγαν.

ΚΡ. ἦ μὴν κελεύσω κἀπιθωύξω γε πρός.

6   ΑΙΣΧΥΛΟΥ

χώρει κάτω, σκέλη δὲ κίρκωσον βίᾳ.
ΗΦ. καὶ δὴ πέπρακται τοὔργον οὐ μακρῷ πόνῳ.   75
ΚΡ. ἐρρωμένως νῦν θεῖνε διατόρους πέδας·
ὡς οὑπιτιμητής γε τῶν ἔργων βαρύς.
ΗΦ. ὅμοια μορφῇ γλῶσσά σου γηρύεται.
ΚΡ. σὺ μαλθακίζου, τὴν δ' ἐμὴν αὐθαδίαν
ὀργῆς τε τραχύτητα μὴ 'πίπλησσέ μοι.   80
ΗΦ. στείχωμεν· ὡς κώλοισιν ἀμφίβληστρ' ἔχει. [Exit.
ΚΡ. [To PROMETHEUS]
ἐνταῦθα νῦν ὕβριζε καὶ θεῶν γέρα
συλῶν ἐφημέροισι προστίθει. τί σοι
οἷοί τε θνητοὶ τῶνδ' ἀπαντλῆσαι πόνων;
ψευδωνύμως σε δαίμονες Προμηθέα   85
καλοῦσιν· αὐτὸν γάρ σε δεῖ προμηθέως,
ὅτῳ τρόπῳ τῆσδ' ἐκκυλισθήσῃ τέχνης.
[Exeunt CRATOS and BIA, following HEPHAESTUS.
PROMETHEUS remains chained to the rock alone.]
ΠΡ. Ὦ δῖος αἰθὴρ καὶ ταχύπτεροι πνοαί,
ποταμῶν τε πηγαὶ ποντίων τε κυμάτων
ἀνήριθμον γέλασμα, παμμῆτόρ τε γῆ,   90
καὶ τὸν πανόπτην κύκλον ἡλίου καλῶ·
ἴδεσθέ μ' οἷα πρὸς θεῶν πάσχω θεός.
δέρχθηθ' οἵαις αἰκίαισιν
διακναιόμενος τὸν μυριετῆ
χρόνον ἀθλεύσω· τοιόνδ' ὁ νέος   95
ταγὸς μακάρων ἐξηῦρ' ἐπ' ἐμοὶ
δεσμὸν ἀεικῆ.
φεῦ φεῦ, τὸ παρὸν τό τ' ἐπερχόμενον
πῆμα στενάχω, πῇ ποτε μόχθων
χρὴ τέρματα τῶνδ' ἐπιτεῖλαι.   100
καίτοι τί φημι; πάντα προυξεπίσταμαι

σκεθρῶς τὰ μέλλοντ', οὐδέ μοι ποταίνιον
πῆμ' οὐδὲν ἥξει. τὴν πεπρωμένην δὲ χρὴ
αἶσαν φέρειν ὡς ῥᾷστα, γιγνώσκονθ' ὅτι
τὸ τῆς ἀνάγκης ἔστ' ἀδήριτον σθένος.   105
ἀλλ' οὔτε σιγᾶν οὔτε μὴ σιγᾶν τύχας
οἷόν τέ μοι τάσδ' ἐστί. θνητοῖς γὰρ γέρα
πορὼν ἀνάγκαις ταῖσδ' ἐνέζευγμαι τάλας·
ναρθηκοπλήρωτον δὲ θηρῶμαι πυρὸς
πηγὴν κλοπαίαν, ἢ διδάσκαλος τέχνης   110
πάσης βροτοῖς πέφηνε καὶ μέγας πόρος.
τοιῶνδε ποινὰς ἀμπλακημάτων τίνω
ὑπαίθριος δεσμοῖς *πεπασσαλευμένος.

Ἆ ἆ, ἔα ἔα.
τίς ἀχώ, τίς ὀδμὰ   115
προσέπτα μ' ἀφεγγής,   (115)
θεόσυτος, ἢ βρότειος, ἢ κεκραμένη;
τερμόνιον ἵκετ' ἐπὶ πάγον
πόνων ἐμῶν θεωρός, ἢ τί δὴ θέλων;
ὁρᾶτε δεσμώτην με δύσποτμον θεόν,   120
τὸν Διὸς ἐχθρὸν, τὸν πᾶσι θεοῖς   (120)
δι' ἀπεχθείας ἐλθόνθ' ὁπόσοι
τὴν Διὸς αὐλὴν εἰσοιχνεῦσιν,
διὰ τὴν λίαν φιλότητα βροτῶν.
φεῦ φεῦ, τί ποτ' αὖ κινάθισμα κλύω   125
πέλας οἰωνῶν;   (125)
αἰθὴρ δ' ἐλαφραῖς πτερύγων ῥιπαῖς
ὑποσυρίζει.
πᾶν μοι φοβερὸν τὸ προσέρπον.

8　ΑΙΣΧΥΛΟΥ

[Πάροδος. *Enter* CHORUS OF OCEAN-NYMPHS *in a winged car.*]

ΧΟ.　Μηδὲν φοβηθῇς·　　　　　　　　　　[Στρ. α'. 130
　　φιλία γὰρ ἅδε τάξις
　　πτερύγων θοαῖς ἁμίλλαις
　　προσέβα τόνδε πάγον, πατρῴας　　　　　　(130)
　　μόγις παρειποῦσα φρένας·
　　κραιπνοφόροι δέ μ' ἔπεμψαν αὖραι.　　　135
　　κτύπου γὰρ ἀχὼ
　　χάλυβος διῆξεν ἄντρων
　　μυχόν, ἐκ δ' ἔπληξέ μου τὰν
　　θεμερῶπιν αἰδῶ·
　　σύθην δ' ἀπέδιλος ὄχῳ πτερωτῷ.　　　140 (135

ΠΡ.　αἰαῖ αἰαῖ,
　　τῆς πολυτέκνου Τηθύος ἔκγονα
　　τοῦ περὶ πᾶσάν θ' εἱλισσομένου
　　χθόν' ἀκοιμήτῳ ῥεύματι παῖδες
　　πατρὸς Ὠκεανοῦ,　　　　　　　　145 (140]
　　δέρχθητ', ἐσίδεσθ' οἵῳ δεσμῷ
　　προσπορπατὸς τῆσδε φάραγγος
　　σκοπέλοισιν ἄκροις
　　φρουρὰν ἄζηλον ὀχήσω.

ΧΟ.　λεύσσω, Προμηθεῦ·　　　　　　　['Αντ. α'. 150
　　φοβερὰ δ' ἐμοῖσιν ὄσσοις
　　ὀμίχλα προσῇξε πλήρης
　　δακρύων σὸν δέμας εἰσιδοῦσαν　　　　　(145)
　　πέτραις προσαυαινόμενον
　　ταῖσδ' ἀδαμαντοδέτοισι λύμαις.　　　155
　　νέοι γὰρ οἰα-
　　κονόμοι κρατοῦσ' Ὀλύμπου·

νεοχμοῖς δὲ δὴ νόμοις Ζεὺς
ἀθέτως κρατύνει, (150)
τὰ πρὶν δὲ πελώρια νῦν ἀιστοῖ. 160

ΠΡ. εἰ γάρ μ' ὑπὸ γῆν νέρθεν θ' Ἅιδου
τοῦ νεκροδέγμονος εἰς ἀπέραντον
Τάρταρον ἧκεν,
δεσμοῖς ἀλύτοις ἀγρίοις πελάσας, (155)
ὡς μήτε θεὸς μήτε τις ἄλλος 165
τοῖσδ' ἐπεγήθει·
νῦν δ' αἰθέριον κίνυγμ' ὁ τάλας
ἐχθροῖς ἐπίχαρτα πέπονθα.

ΧΟ. τίς ὧδε τλησικάρδιος [Στρ. β'.
θεῶν, ὅτῳ τάδ' ἐπιχαρῇ; 170 (160)
τίς οὐ ξυνασχαλᾷ κακοῖς
τεοῖσι, δίχα γε Διός; ὁ δ'
ἐπικότως ἀεὶ
θέμενος ἄγναμπτον νόον
δάμναται Οὐρανίαν 175 (165)
γένναν, οὐδὲ λή-
ξει, πρὶν ἂν ἢ κορέσῃ κέαρ,
ἢ παλάμᾳ τινὶ
τὰν δυσάλωτον ἕλῃ τις ἀρχάν.

ΠΡ. ἦ μὴν ἔτ' ἐμοῦ, καίπερ κρατεραῖς 180
ἐν γυιοπέδαις αἰκιζομένου,
χρείαν ἕξει μακάρων πρύτανις,
δεῖξαι τὸ νέον βούλευμ' ἀφ' ὅτου (170)
σκῆπτρον τιμάς τ' ἀποσυλᾶται.
καί μ' οὔτε μελιγλώσσοις πειθοῦς 185
ἐπαοιδαῖσιν θέλξει, στερεάς τ'
οὔποτ' ἀπειλὰς πτήξας τόδ' ἐγὼ

καταμηνύσω, πρὶν ἂν ἐξ ἀγρίων (175)
δεσμῶν χαλάσῃ ποινάς τε τίνειν
τῆσδ᾽ αἰκίας ἐθελήσῃ. 190

ΧΟ. σὺ μὲν θρασύς τε καὶ πικραῖς [Ἀντ. β΄.
δύαισιν οὐδὲν ἐπιχαλᾷς,
ἄγαν δ᾽ ἐλευθεροστομεῖς. (180)
ἐμὰς δὲ φρένας ἐρέθισε
διάτορος φόβος· 195
δέδια δ᾽ ἀμφὶ σαῖς τύχαις,
πᾷ ποτε τῶνδε πόνων
χρή σε τέρμα κέλ-
σαντ᾽ ἐσιδεῖν· ἀκίχητα γὰρ
ἤθεα καὶ κέαρ 200
ἀπαράμυθον ἔχει Κρόνου παῖς. (185)

ΠΡ. οἶδ᾽ ὅτι τραχὺς καὶ παρ᾽ ἑαυτῷ
τὸ δίκαιον ἔχων [Ζεύς]· [ἀλλ᾽] ἔμπας, οἴω,
μαλακογνώμων
ἔσται ποθ᾽, ὅταν ταύτῃ ῥαισθῇ· 205
τὴν δ᾽ ἀτέραμνον στορέσας ὀργὴν (190)
εἰς ἀρθμὸν ἐμοὶ καὶ φιλότητα
σπεύδων σπεύδοντί ποθ᾽ ἥξει.

[Πρῶτον Ἐπεισόδιον.]

ΧΟ. Πάντ᾽ ἐκκάλυψον καὶ γέγων᾽ ἡμῖν λόγον,
ποίῳ λαβών σε Ζεὺς ἐπ᾽ αἰτιάματι 210
οὕτως ἀτίμως καὶ πικρῶς αἰκίζεται· (195)
δίδαξον ἡμᾶς, εἴ τι μὴ βλάπτῃ λόγῳ.

ΠΡ. ἀλγεινὰ μέν μοι καὶ λέγειν ἐστὶν τάδε,
ἄλγος δὲ σιγᾶν, πανταχῇ δὲ δύσποτμα.
   ἐπεὶ τάχιστ᾽ ἤρξαντο δαίμονες χόλου 215
στάσις τ᾽ ἐν ἀλλήλοισιν ὠροθύνετο, (200)

οἱ μὲν θέλοντες ἐκβαλεῖν ἕδρας Κρόνον,
ὡς Ζεὺς ἀνάσσοι δῆθεν, οἱ δὲ τοὔμπαλιν
σπεύδοντες, ὡς Ζεὺς μήποτ᾽ ἄρξειεν θεῶν,
ἐνταῦθ᾽ ἐγὼ τὰ λῷστα βουλεύων πιθεῖν   220
Τιτᾶνας, Οὐρανοῦ τε καὶ Χθονὸς τέκνα,   (205)
οὐκ ἠδυνήθην· αἱμύλας δὲ μηχανὰς
ἀτιμάσαντες καρτεροῖς φρονήμασιν
ᾤοντ᾽ ἀμοχθὶ πρὸς βίαν τε δεσπόσειν.
ἐμοὶ δὲ μήτηρ οὐχ ἅπαξ μόνον Θέμις   225
καὶ Γαῖα, πολλῶν ὀνομάτων μορφὴ μία,   (210)
τὸ μέλλον ᾗ κραίνοιτο προυτεθεσπίκει,
ὡς οὐ κατ᾽ ἰσχὺν οὐδὲ πρὸς τὸ καρτερὸν
χρείη, δόλῳ δὲ τοὺς ὑπερσχόντας κρατεῖν.
τοιαῦτ᾽ ἐμοῦ λόγοισιν ἐξηγουμένου   230
οὐκ ἠξίωσαν οὐδὲ προσβλέψαι τὸ πᾶν.   (215)
κράτιστα δή μοι τῶν παρεστώτων τότε
ἐφαίνετ᾽ εἶναι προσλαβόντι μητέρα
ἑκόνθ᾽ ἑκόντι Ζηνὶ συμπαραστατεῖν.
ἐμαῖς δὲ βουλαῖς Ταρτάρου μελαμβαθὴς   235
κευθμὼν καλύπτει τὸν παλαιγενῆ Κρόνον   (220)
αὐτοῖσι συμμάχοισι. τοιάδ᾽ ἐξ ἐμοῦ
ὁ τῶν θεῶν τύραννος ὠφελημένος
κακαῖσι ποιναῖς ταῖσδέ μ᾽ ἐξημείψατο.
ἔνεστι γάρ πως τοῦτο τῇ τυραννίδι   240
νόσημα, τοῖς φίλοισι μὴ πεποιθέναι.   (225)
    ὃ δ᾽ οὖν ἐρωτᾶτ᾽, αἰτίαν καθ᾽ ἥντινα
αἰκίζεταί με, τοῦτο δὴ σαφηνιῶ.
    ὅπως τάχιστα τὸν πατρῷον ἐς θρόνον
καθέζετ᾽, εὐθὺς δαίμοσιν νέμει γέρα   245
ἄλλοισιν ἄλλα, καὶ διεστοιχίζετο   (230)
ἀρχήν, βροτῶν δὲ τῶν ταλαιπώρων λόγον

οὐκ ἔσχεν οὐδέν, ἀλλ᾽ ἀϊστώσας γένος
τὸ πᾶν ἔχρῃζεν ἄλλο φιτῦσαι νέον.
καὶ τοῖσιν οὐδεὶς ἀντέβαινε πλὴν ἐμοῦ.   250
ἐγὼ δ᾽ ἐτόλμησ᾽· ἐξελυσάμην βροτοὺς   (235)
τὸ μὴ διαρραισθέντας εἰς Ἅιδου μολεῖν.
τῷ τοι τοιαῖσδε πημοναῖσι κάμπτομαι,
πάσχειν μὲν ἀλγειναῖσιν, οἰκτραῖσιν δ᾽ ἰδεῖν·
θνητοὺς δ᾽ ἐν οἴκτῳ προθέμενος, τούτου τυχεῖν 255
οὐκ ἠξιώθην αὐτός, ἀλλὰ νηλεῶς   (240)
ὧδ᾽ ἐρρύθμισμαι, Ζηνὶ δυσκλεὴς θέα.

ΧΟ. σιδηρόφρων τε κἀκ πέτρας εἰργασμένος
ὅστις, Προμηθεῦ, σοῖσιν οὐ συνασχαλᾷ
μόχθοις· ἐγὼ γὰρ οὔτ᾽ ἂν εἰσιδεῖν τάδε   260
ἔχρῃζον, εἰσιδοῦσά τ᾽ ἠλγύνθην κέαρ.   (245)

ΠΡ. καὶ μὴν φίλοις ἐλεινὸς εἰσορᾶν ἐγώ.

ΧΟ. μή πού τι προύβης τῶνδε καὶ περαιτέρω;

ΠΡ. θνητούς γ᾽ ἔπαυσα μὴ προδέρκεσθαι μόρον.

ΧΟ. τὸ ποῖον εὑρὼν τῆσδε φάρμακον νόσου;   265

ΠΡ. τυφλὰς ἐν αὐτοῖς ἐλπίδας κατῴκισα.   (250)

ΧΟ. μέγ᾽ ὠφέλημα τοῦτ᾽ ἐδωρήσω βροτοῖς.

ΠΡ. πρὸς τοῖσδε μέντοι πῦρ ἐγώ σφιν ὤπασα.

ΧΟ. καὶ νῦν φλογωπὸν πῦρ ἔχουσ᾽ ἐφήμεροι;

ΠΡ. ἀφ᾽ οὗ γε πολλὰς ἐκμαθήσονται τέχνας.   270

ΧΟ. τοιοῖσδε δή σε Ζεὺς ἐπ᾽ αἰτιάμασιν—   (255)

ΠΡ. αἰκίζεταί τε κοὐδαμῇ χαλᾷ κακῶν.

ΧΟ. οὐδ᾽ ἔστιν ἄθλου τέρμα σοι προκείμενον;

ΠΡ. οὐκ ἄλλο γ᾽ οὐδέν, πλὴν ὅταν κείνῳ δοκῇ.

ΧΟ. δόξει δὲ πῶς; τίς ἐλπίς; οὐχ ὁρᾷς ὅτι   275
ἥμαρτες; ὡς δ᾽ ἥμαρτες οὔτ᾽ ἐμοὶ λέγειν   (260)
καθ᾽ ἡδονὴν σοί τ᾽ ἄλγος. ἀλλὰ ταῦτα μὲν
μεθῶμεν, ἄθλου δ᾽ ἔκλυσιν ζήτει τινά.

ΠΡ. ἐλαφρὸν, ὅστις πημάτων ἔξω πόδα
ἔχει, παραινεῖν νουθετεῖν τε τὸν κακῶς 280
πράσσοντ᾽· ἐγὼ δὲ ταῦθ᾽ ἅπαντ᾽ ἠπιστάμην· (265)
ἑκών, ἑκών—ἥμαρτον, οὐκ ἀρνήσομαι—
θνητοῖς ἀρήγων αὐτὸς ηὑρόμην πόνους·
οὐ μήν τι ποιναῖς γ᾽ ᾠόμην τοίαισί με
κατισχνανεῖσθαι πρὸς πέτραις πεδαρσίοις, 285
τυχόντ᾽ ἐρήμου τοῦδ᾽ ἀγείτονος πάγου. (270)
καί μοι τὰ μὲν παρόντα μὴ δύρεσθ᾽ ἄχη,
πέδοι δὲ βᾶσαι τὰς προσερπούσας τύχας
ἀκούσαθ᾽, ὡς μάθητε διὰ τέλους τὸ πᾶν.
πίθεσθέ μοι, πίθεσθε, συμπονήσατε 290
τῷ νῦν μογοῦντι. ταυτά τοι πλανωμένη (275)
πρὸς ἄλλοτ᾽ ἄλλον πημονὴ προσιζάνει.
ΧΟ. οὐκ ἀκούσαις ἐπεθώυξας
τοῦτο, Προμηθεῦ.
καὶ νῦν ἐλαφρῷ ποδὶ κραιπνόσυτον 295
θᾶκον προλιποῦσ᾽ αἰθέρα θ᾽ ἁγνὸν (280)
πόρον οἰωνῶν, ὀκριοέσσῃ
χθονὶ τῇδε πελῶ· τοὺς σοὺς δὲ πόνους
χρῄζω διὰ παντὸς ἀκοῦσαι.

[*They descend from their car into the Orchestra. Enter*
OCEANUS *on a winged horse.*]

ΩΚ. Ἥκω δολιχῆς τέρμα κελεύθου 300
διαμειψάμενος πρὸς σέ, Προμηθεῦ, (285)
τὸν πτερυγωκῆ τόνδ᾽ οἰωνὸν
γνώμῃ στομίων ἄτερ εὐθύνων·
ταῖς σαῖς δὲ τύχαις, ἴσθι, συναλγῶ.
τό τε γάρ με, δοκῶ, ξυγγενὲς οὕτως 305

14   ΑΙΣΧΥΛΟΥ

ἐσαναγκάζει, χωρίς τε γένους   (290)
οὐκ ἔστιν ὅτῳ μείζονα μοῖραν
νείμαιμ' ἢ σοί.
γνώσῃ δὲ τάδ' ὡς ἔτυμ', οὐδὲ μάτην
χαριτογλωσσεῖν ἔνι μοι· φέρε γὰρ   310
σήμαιν' ὅ τι χρή σοι συμπράσσειν·   (295)
οὐ γάρ ποτ' ἐρεῖς ὡς Ὠκεανοῦ
φίλος ἐστὶ βεβαιότερός σοι.

ΠΡ. ἔα, τί χρῆμα; καὶ σὺ δὴ πόνων ἐμῶν
ἥκεις ἐπόπτης; πῶς ἐτόλμησας, λιπὼν   315
ἐπώνυμόν τε ῥεῦμα καὶ πετρηρεφῆ   (300)
αὐτόκτιτ' ἄντρα, τὴν σιδηρομήτορα
ἐλθεῖν ἐς αἶαν; ἦ θεωρήσων τύχας
ἐμὰς ἀφῖξαι καὶ συνασχαλῶν κακοῖς;
δέρκου θέαμα, τόνδε τὸν Διὸς φίλον,   320
τὸν συγκαταστήσαντα τὴν τυραννίδα,   (305)
οἵαις ὑπ' αὐτοῦ πημοναῖσι κάμπτομαι.

ΩΚ. ὁρῶ, Προμηθεῦ, καὶ παραινέσαι γέ σοι
θέλω τὰ λῷστα, καίπερ ὄντι ποικίλῳ.
γίγνωσκε σαυτὸν καὶ μεθάρμοσαι τρόπους   325
νέους· νέος γὰρ καὶ τύραννος ἐν θεοῖς.   (310)
εἰ δ' ὧδε τραχεῖς καὶ τεθηγμένους λόγους
ῥίψεις, τάχ' ἄν σου καὶ μακρὰν ἀνωτέρω
θακῶν κλύοι Ζεύς, ὥστε σοι τὸν νῦν *ὄχλον
παρόντα μόχθων παιδιὰν εἶναι δοκεῖν.   330
ἀλλ', ὦ ταλαίπωρ', ἃς ἔχεις ὀργὰς ἄφες,   (315)
ζήτει δὲ τῶνδε πημάτων ἀπαλλαγάς.
ἀρχαῖ' ἴσως σοι φαίνομαι λέγειν τάδε·
τοιαῦτα μέντοι τῆς ἄγαν ὑψηγόρου
γλώσσης, Προμηθεῦ, τἀπίχειρα γίγνεται.   335
σὺ δ' οὐδέπω ταπεινὸς οὐδ' εἴκεις κακοῖς,   (320)

πρὸς τοῖς παροῦσι δ' ἄλλα προσλαβεῖν θέλεις.
οὔκουν ἔμοιγε χρώμενος διδασκάλῳ
πρὸς κέντρα κῶλον ἐκτενεῖς, ὁρῶν ὅτι
τραχὺς μόναρχος οὐδ' ὑπεύθυνος κρατεῖ. 340
καὶ νῦν ἐγὼ μὲν εἶμι καὶ πειράσομαι (3×5)
ἐὰν δύνωμαι τῶνδέ σ' ἐκλῦσαι πόνων·
σὺ δ' ἡσύχαζε μηδ' ἄγαν λαβροστόμει.
ἢ οὐκ οἶσθ', ἀκριβῶς ὢν περισσόφρων, ὅτι
γλώσσῃ ματαίᾳ ζημία προστρίβεται; 345
ΠΡ. ζηλῶ σ' ὁθούνεκ' ἐκτὸς αἰτίας κυρεῖς, (330)
πάντων μετασχὼν καὶ τετολμηκὼς ἐμοί.
καὶ νῦν ἔασον μηδέ σοι μελησάτω.
πάντως γὰρ οὐ πείσεις νιν· οὐ γὰρ εὐπιθής.
πάπταινε δ' αὐτὸς μή τι πημανθῇς ὁδῷ. 350
ΩΚ. πολλῷ γ' ἀμείνων τοὺς πέλας φρενοῦν ἔφυς (335)
ἢ σαυτόν· ἔργῳ κοὐ λόγῳ τεκμαίρομαι.
ὁρμώμενον δὲ μηδαμῶς ἀντισπάσῃς·
αὐχῶ γὰρ, αὐχῶ τήνδε δωρειὰν ἐμοὶ
δώσειν Δί', ὥστε τῶνδέ σ' ἐκλῦσαι πόνων. 355
ΠΡ. τὰ μέν σ' ἐπαινῶ κοὐδαμῇ λήξω ποτέ· (340)
προθυμίας γὰρ οὐδὲν ἐλλείπεις. ἀτὰρ
μηδὲν πόνει· μάτην γὰρ, οὐδὲν ὠφελῶν
ἐμοὶ, πονήσεις, εἴ τι καὶ πονεῖν θέλεις.
ἀλλ' ἡσύχαζε σαυτὸν ἐκποδὼν ἔχων· 360
ἐγὼ γὰρ οὐκ, εἰ δυστυχῶ, τοῦδ' εἵνεκα (345)
θέλοιμ' ἂν ὡς πλείστοισι πημονὰς τυχεῖν.
οὐ δῆτ', ἐπεί με χαὶ κασιγνήτου τύχαι
τείρουσ' Ἄτλαντος, ὃς πρὸς ἑσπέρους τόπους
ἕστηκε κίον' οὐρανοῦ τε καὶ χθονὸς 365
ὤμοις ἐρείδων, ἄχθος οὐκ εὐάγκαλον. (350)
τὸν γηγενῆ τε Κιλικίων οἰκήτορα

ἄντρων ἰδὼν ᾤκτειρα, δάιον τέρας,
ἑκατογκάρανον πρὸς βίαν χειρούμενον
Τυφῶνα θοῦρον· †πᾶσιν ὃς ἀντέστη θεοῖς, 370
σμερδναῖσι γαμφηλαῖσι συρίζων φόβον· (355)
ἐξ ὀμμάτων δ᾽ ἤστραπτε γοργωπὸν σέλας,
ὡς τὴν Διὸς τυραννίδ᾽ ἐκπέρσων βίᾳ.
ἀλλ᾽ ἦλθεν αὐτῷ Ζηνὸς ἄγρυπνον βέλος,
καταιβάτης κεραυνὸς ἐκπνέων φλόγα, 375
ὃς αὐτὸν ἐξέπληξε τῶν ὑψηγόρων (360)
κομπασμάτων· φρένας γὰρ εἰς αὐτὰς τυπεὶς
ἐφεψαλώθη κἀξεβροντήθη σθένος.
καὶ νῦν ἀχρεῖον καὶ παράορον δέμας
κεῖται στενωποῦ πλησίον θαλασσίου 380
ἰπούμενος ῥίζαισιν Αἰτναίαις ὕπο, (365)
κορυφαῖς δ᾽ ἐν ἄκραις ἥμενος μυδροκτυπεῖ
Ἥφαιστος. ἔνθεν ἐκραγήσονταί ποτε
ποταμοὶ πυρὸς δάπτοντες ἀγρίαις γνάθοις
τῆς καλλικάρπου Σικελίας λευροὺς γύας· 385
τοιόνδε Τυφὼς ἐξαναζέσει χόλον (370)
θερμοῖς *ἀπλάτου βέλεσι πυρπνόου ζάλης,
καίπερ κεραυνῷ Ζηνὸς ἠνθρακωμένος.
σὺ δ᾽ οὐκ ἄπειρος, οὐδ᾽ ἐμοῦ διδασκάλου
χρῄζεις· σεαυτὸν σῷζ᾽ ὅπως ἐπίστασαι· 390
ἐγὼ δὲ τὴν παροῦσαν ἀντλήσω τύχην, (375)
ἔστ᾽ ἂν Διὸς φρόνημα λωφήσῃ χόλου.
ΩΚ. οὔκουν, Προμηθεῦ, τοῦτο γιγνώσκεις, ὅτι
ὀργῆς νοσούσης εἰσὶν ἰατροὶ λόγοι;
ΠΡ. ἐάν τις ἐν καιρῷ γε μαλθάσσῃ κέαρ 395
καὶ μὴ σφριγῶντα θυμὸν ἰσχναίνῃ βίᾳ. (380)
ΩΚ. ἐν τῷ προθυμεῖσθαι δὲ καὶ τολμᾶν τίνα
ὁρᾷς ἐνοῦσαν ζημίαν; δίδασκέ με.

ΠΡ. μόχθον περισσὸν κουφόνουν τ' εὐηθίαν.

ΩΚ. ἔα με τῇδε τῇ νόσῳ νοσεῖν, ἐπεὶ   400
   κέρδιστον εὖ φρονοῦντα μὴ φρονεῖν δοκεῖν.   (385)

ΠΡ. ἐμὸν δοκήσει τἀμπλάκημ' εἶναι τόδε.

ΩΚ. σαφῶς μ' ἐς οἶκον σὸς λόγος στέλλει πάλιν.

ΠΡ. μὴ γάρ σε θρῆνος οὑμὸς εἰς ἔχθραν βάλῃ.

ΩΚ. ἢ τῷ νέον θακοῦντι παγκρατεῖς ἕδρας;   405

ΠΡ. τούτου φυλάσσου μή ποτ' ἀχθεσθῇ κέαρ.   (390)

ΩΚ. ἡ σή, Προμηθεῦ, συμφορὰ διδάσκαλος.

ΠΡ. στέλλου, κομίζου, σῷζε τὸν παρόντα νοῦν.

ΩΚ. ὁρμωμένῳ μοι τόνδ' ἐθώυξας λόγον.
   λευρὸν γὰρ οἶμον αἰθέρος ψαίρει πτεροῖς   410
   τετρασκελὴς οἰωνός· ἄσμενος δέ τἂν   (395)
   σταθμοῖς ἐν οἰκείοισι κάμψειεν γόνυ.   [*Exit*.

     [Πρῶτον Στάσιμον.]

ΧΟ. Στένω σε τᾶς οὐ-   [Στρ. α'.
   λομένας τύχας, Προμηθεῦ·
   δακρυσίστακτον [δ'] ἀπ' ὄσσων   415
   ῥαδινὸν λειβομένα ῥέος παρειὰν   (400)
   νοτίοις ἔτεγξα παγαῖς.
   ἀμέγαρτα γὰρ τάδε Ζεὺς
   ἰδίοις νόμοις κρατύνων
   ὑπερήφανον θεοῖς τοῖς   420
   πάρος ἐνδείκνυσιν αἰχμάν.   (405)

   πρόπασα δ' ἤδη   ['Αντ. α'.
   στονόεν λέλακε χώρα,
   μεγαλοσχήμονά τ' ἀρχαι-
   οπρεπῆ <‒ ◡ ◡ ‒> στένουσι τὰν σὰν   425
   ξυνομαιμόνων τε τιμάν,
   ὁπόσοι τ' ἔποικον ἁγνᾶς   (410)

'Ασίας ἔδος νέμονται,
μεγαλοστόνοισι σοῖς πή-
μασι συγκάμνουσι θνατοί,   430

Κολχίδος τε γᾶς ἔνοικοι   [Στρ. β'. (415)
παρθένοι, μάχας ἄτρεστοι,
καὶ Σκύθης ὅμιλος, οἳ γᾶς
ἔσχατον τόπον ἀμφὶ Μαι-
ῶτιν ἔχουσι λίμναν,   435

'Αραβίας τ' ἄρειον ἄνθος,   ['Αντ. β'. (420)
ὑψίκρημνόν [θ'] οἳ πόλισμα
Καυκάσου πέλας νέμουσιν,
δάιος στρατὸς, ὀξυπρώ-
ροισι βρέμων ἐν αἰχμαῖς.   440

μόνον δὴ πρόσθεν ἄλλον ἐν πόνοις   ['Επῳδ.
δαμέντ' [ἀδαμαντοδέτοις
Τιτᾶνα λύμαις] εἰσιδόμαν θεόν,   (426)
Ἄτλανθ', †ὃς αἰὲν ὑπέροχον σθένος
κραταιὸν οὐράνιόν τε πόλον   445
νώτοις ὑποστενάζει.   (430)
βοᾷ δὲ πόντιος κλύδων
ξυμπίτνων, στένει βυθός,
κελαινὸς [δ'] Ἄιδος ὑποβρέμει μυχὸς γᾶς,
παγαί θ' ἀγνορύτων ποταμῶν   450
στένουσιν ἄλγος οἰκτρόν.   (435)

[Δεύτερον Ἐπεισόδιον.]

ΠΡ. Μή τοι χλιδῇ δοκεῖτε μηδ' αὐθαδίᾳ
σιγᾶν με· συννοίᾳ δὲ δάπτομαι κέαρ,
ὁρῶν ἐμαυτὸν ὧδε *προυσελούμενον.

καίτοι θεοῖσι τοῖς νέοις τούτοις γέρα   455
τίς ἄλλος ἢ 'γὼ παντελῶς διώρισεν;   (440)
ἀλλ' αὐτὰ σιγῶ· καὶ γὰρ εἰδυίαισιν ἂν
ὑμῖν λέγοιμι· τὰν βροτοῖς δὲ πήματα
ἀκούσαθ', ὥς σφας νηπίους ὄντας τὸ πρὶν
ἔννους ἔθηκα καὶ φρενῶν ἐπηβόλους.   460
λέξω δὲ, μέμψιν οὔτιν' ἀνθρώποις ἔχων,   (445)
ἀλλ' ὧν δέδωκ' εὔνοιαν ἐξηγούμενος·
   οἳ πρῶτα μὲν βλέποντες ἔβλεπον μάτην,
κλύοντες οὐκ ἤκουον, ἀλλ' ὀνειράτων
ἀλίγκιοι μορφαῖσι τὸν μακρὸν βίον   465
ἔφυρον εἰκῇ πάντα· κοὔτε πλινθυφεῖς   (450)
δόμους προσείλους ᾖσαν, οὐ ξυλουργίαν,
κατώρυχες δ' ἔναιον, ὥστ' ἀήσυροι
μύρμηκες, ἄντρων ἐν μυχοῖς ἀνηλίοις.
ἦν δ' οὐδὲν αὐτοῖς οὔτε χείματος τέκμαρ   470
οὔτ' ἀνθεμώδους ἦρος οὔτε καρπίμου   (455)
θέρους βέβαιον, ἀλλ' ἄτερ γνώμης τὸ πᾶν
ἔπρασσον, ἔστε δή σφιν ἀντολὰς ἐγὼ
ἄστρων ἔδειξα τάς τε δυσκρίτους δύσεις.
καὶ μὴν ἀριθμὸν, ἔξοχον σοφισμάτων,   475
ἐξηῦρον αὐτοῖς, γραμμάτων τε συνθέσεις,   (460)
μνήμην ἁπάντων, μουσομήτορ' ἐργάνην.
κἄζευξα πρῶτος ἐν ζυγοῖσι κνώδαλα
ζεύγλαισι δουλεύοντα, σώμασίν θ' ὅπως
θνητοῖς μεγίστων διάδοχοι μοχθημάτων   480
γένοινθ', ὑφ' ἅρμα τ' ἤγαγον φιληνίους   (465)
ἵππους, ἄγαλμα τῆς ὑπερπλούτου χλιδῆς.
θαλασσόπλαγκτα δ' οὔτις ἄλλος ἀντ' ἐμοῦ
λινόπτερ' ηὗρε ναυτίλων ὀχήματα.
   τοιαῦτα μηχανήματ' ἐξευρὼν τάλας   485

20 ΑΙΣΧΥΛΟΥ

βροτοῖσιν αὐτὸς οὐκ ἔχω σόφισμ' ὅτῳ (470)
τῆς νῦν παρούσης πημονῆς ἀπαλλαγῶ.

ΧΟ. πέπονθας αἰκὲς πῆμ'· ἀποσφαλεὶς φρενῶν
πλανᾷ, κακὸς δ' ἰατρὸς ὥς τις ἐς νόσον
πεσὼν ἀθυμεῖς καὶ σεαυτὸν οὐκ ἔχεις 490
εὑρεῖν ὁποίοις φαρμάκοις ἰάσιμος. (475)

ΠΡ. τὰ λοιπά μου κλύουσα θαυμάσει πλέον,
οἵας τέχνας τε καὶ πόρους ἐμησάμην.
τὸ μὲν μέγιστον, εἴ τις ἐς νόσον πέσοι,
οὐκ ἦν ἀλέξημ' οὐδέν, οὔτε βρώσιμον, 495
οὐ χριστόν, οὐδὲ πιστόν, ἀλλὰ φαρμάκων (480)
χρείᾳ κατεσκέλλοντο, πρίν γ' ἐγώ σφισιν
ἔδειξα κράσεις ἠπίων ἀκεσμάτων,
αἷς τὰς ἁπάσας ἐξαμύνονται νόσους.
τρόπους τε πολλοὺς μαντικῆς ἐστοίχισα, 500
κἄκρινα πρῶτος ἐξ ὀνειράτων ἃ χρὴ (485)
ὕπαρ γενέσθαι, κληδόνας τε δυσκρίτους
ἐγνώρισ' αὐτοῖς ἐνοδίους τε συμβόλους.
γαμψωνύχων τε πτῆσιν οἰωνῶν σκεθρῶς
διώρισ', οἵτινές τε δεξιοὶ φύσιν 505
εὐωνύμους τε, καὶ δίαιταν ἥντινα (490)
ἔχουσ' ἕκαστοι, καὶ πρὸς ἀλλήλους τίνες
ἔχθραι τε καὶ στέργηθρα καὶ συνεδρίαι·
σπλάγχνων τε λειότητα, καὶ χροιὰν τίνα
ἔχοντ' ἂν εἴη δαίμοσιν πρὸς ἡδονήν, 510
χολῆς λοβοῦ τε ποικίλην εὐμορφίαν. (495)
κνίσῃ τε κῶλα συγκαλυπτὰ καὶ μακρὰν
ὀσφῦν πυρώσας δυστέκμαρτον ἐς τέχνην
ὥδωσα θνητούς, καὶ φλογωπὰ σήματα
ἐξωμμάτωσα, πρόσθεν ὄντ' ἐπάργεμα. 515
τοιαῦτα μὲν δὴ ταῦτ'· ἔνερθε δὲ χθονὸς (500)

κεκρυμμέν' ἀνθρώποισιν ὠφελήματα,
χαλκὸν, σίδηρον, ἄργυρον χρυσόν τε τίς
φήσειεν ἂν πάροιθεν ἐξευρεῖν ἐμοῦ;
οὐδεὶς, σάφ' οἶδα, μὴ μάτην φλύσαι θέλων. 520
βραχεῖ δὲ μύθῳ πάντα συλλήβδην μάθε, (505)
πᾶσαι τέχναι βροτοῖσιν ἐκ Προμηθέως.

ΧΟ. μή νυν βροτοὺς μὲν ὠφέλει καιροῦ πέρα,
σαυτοῦ δ' ἀκήδει δυστυχοῦντος· ὡς ἐγὼ
εὔελπίς εἰμὶ τῶνδέ σ' ἐκ δεσμῶν ἔτι 525
λυθέντα μηδὲν μεῖον ἰσχύσειν Διός. (510)

ΠΡ. οὐ ταῦτα ταύτῃ μοῖρά πω τελεσφόρος
κρᾶναι πέπρωται, μυρίαις δὲ πημοναῖς
δύαις τε καμφθεὶς, ὧδε δεσμὰ φυγγάνω·
τέχνη δ' ἀνάγκης ἀσθενεστέρα μακρῷ. 530

ΧΟ. τίς οὖν ἀνάγκης ἐστὶν οἰακοστρόφος; (515)

ΠΡ. Μοῖραι τρίμορφοι μνήμονές τ' Ἐρινύες.

ΧΟ. τούτων ἄρα Ζεύς ἐστιν ἀσθενέστερος;

ΠΡ. οὔκουν ἂν ἐκφύγοι γε τὴν πεπρωμένην.

ΧΟ. τί γὰρ πέπρωται Ζηνὶ πλὴν ἀεὶ κρατεῖν; 535

ΠΡ. τοῦτ' οὐκέτ' ἂν πύθοιο μηδὲ λιπάρει. (520)

ΧΟ. ἦ πού τι σεμνόν ἐστιν ὃ ξυναμπέχεις.

ΠΡ. ἄλλου λόγου μέμνησθε, τόνδε δ' οὐδαμῶς
καιρὸς γεγωνεῖν, ἀλλὰ συγκαλυπτέος
ὅσον μάλιστα· τόνδε γὰρ σῴζων ἐγὼ 540
δεσμοὺς ἀεικεῖς καὶ δύας ἐκφυγγάνω. (525)

[Δεύτερον Στάσιμον.]

ΧΟ. Μηδάμ' ὁ πάντα νέμων [Στρ. α΄.
θεῖτ' ἐμᾷ γνώμᾳ κράτος ἀν-
τίπαλον Ζεύς,
μηδ' ἐλινύσαιμι θεοὺς ὁσίαις 545

θοίναις ποτινισσομένα   (530)
βουφόνοις παρ' Ὠκεανοῦ πατρὸς ἄ-
σβεστον πόρον,
μηδ' ἀλίτοιμι λόγοις·
ἀλλά μοι τόδ' ἐμμένοι   550
καὶ μήποτ' ἐκτακείη·   (535)

ἡδύ τι θαρσαλέαις   ['Αντ. α'.
τὸν μακρὸν τείνειν βίον ἐλπίσι, φαναῖς
θυμὸν ἀλδαίνουσαν ἐν εὐφροσύναις.   555
φρίσσω δέ σε δερκομένα   (540)
μυρίοις μόχθοις διακναιόμενον
<--◡->.
Ζῆνα γὰρ οὐ τρομέων
†ἰδίᾳ γνώμᾳ σέβῃ
θνατοὺς ἄγαν, Προμηθεῦ.   560

φέρ', ὅπως χάρις *ἁ   [Στρ. β'.
χάρις, ὦ φίλος, εἰ-
πέ, ποῦ τίς ἀλκὰ, τίς ἐφαμερίων   (545)
ἄρηξις; οὐδ' ἐδέρχθης
ὀλιγοδρανίαν ἄκικυν,   565
ἰσόνειρον, ᾇ τὸ φωτῶν
ἀλαὸν γένος ἐμ-
πεποδισμένον; οὔποτε   (550)
τὰν Διὸς ἁρμονίαν
θνατῶν παρεξίασι βουλαί.   570

ἔμαθον τάδε σὰς   ['Αντ. β'.
προσιδοῦσ' ὀλοὰς
τύχας, Προμηθεῦ. τὸ διαμφίδιον
δέ μοι μέλος προσέπτα   (555)

τόδ' ἐκεῖνό θ' ὅτ' ἀμφὶ λουτρὰ 575
καὶ λέχος σὸν ὑμεναίουν
ἰότατι γάμων,
ὅτε τὰν ὁμοπάτριον
[ἔδνοις] ἄγαγες Ἡσιόναν
πιθὼν δάμαρτα κοινόλεκτρον. 580 (560)
            •
[Τρίτον Ἐπεισόδιον. Enter Io in the form of a maiden
            with cow's horns.]

ΙΩ. Τίς γῆ; τί γένος; τίνα φῶ λεύσσειν
τόνδε χαλινοῖς ἐν πετρίνοισιν
χειμαζόμενον;
τίνος ἀμπλακίας ποινὰς ὀλέκῃ;
σήμηνον ὅποι 585
γῆς ἡ μογερὰ πεπλάνημαι. (565)
ἆ ἆ, ἐή,
χρίει τις αὖ με τὰν τάλαιναν οἶστρος·
εἴδωλον Ἀργου γηγενοῦς—ἄλευ', ἆ Δᾶ—φοβοῦμαι
τὸν μυριωπὸν εἰσορῶσα βούταν. 590
ὁ δὲ πορεύεται δόλιον ὄμμ' ἔχων, (570)
ὃν οὐδὲ κατθανόντα γαῖα κεύθει.
ἀλλά με τὰν τάλαιναν ἐξ ἐνέρων περῶν
κυναγετεῖ πλανᾷ τε νῆστιν ἀνὰ τὰν
παραλίαν ψάμμαν. 595
ὑπὸ δὲ κηρόπλαστος ὀτοβεῖ δόναξ [Στρ.
ἀχέτας ὑπνοδόταν νόμον· (575)
ἰὼ ἰὼ πόποι,
†ποῖ μ' ἄγουσι τηλέπλαγκτοι πλάναι;
τί ποτέ μ', ὦ Κρόνιε παῖ, 600
τί ποτε ταῖσδ'
ἐνέζευξας εὑρὼν ἁμαρ-

4—2

τοῦσαν ἐν πημοναῖς, ἐή,
οἰστρηλάτῳ δὲ δείματι δειλαίαν (580)
παράκοπον ὧδε τείρεις;
πυρί <με> φλέξον, ἢ χθονὶ κάλυψον, ἢ 605
ποντίοις δάκεσι δὸς
βορὰν, μηδέ μοι
φθονήσῃς εὐγμάτων, ἄναξ.
ἄδην με πολύπλανοι πλάναι (585)
γεγυμνάκασιν, οὐδ᾽ ἔχω μαθεῖν ὅπᾳ 610
πημονὰς ἀλύξω.
κλύεις φθέγμα τᾶς
βούκερω παρθένου;

ΠΡ. πῶς δ᾽ οὐ κλύω τῆς οἰστροδινήτου κόρης,
τῆς Ἰναχείας; ἢ Διὸς θάλπει κέαρ 615 (590)
ἔρωτι, καὶ νῦν τοὺς ὑπερμήκεις δρόμους
Ἥρᾳ στυγητὸς πρὸς βίαν γυμνάζεται.

ΙΩ. πόθεν ἐμοῦ σὺ πατρὸς ὄνομ᾽ ἀπύεις; ['Αντ.
εἰπέ μοι τᾷ μογερᾷ τίς ὤν,
τίς ἄρα μ᾽, ὦ τάλας, 620
τὰν ταλαίπωρον ὧδ᾽ ἔτυμα προσθροεῖς, (595)
θεόσυτόν τε νόσον ὠ-
νόμασας ἃ μαραίνει με χρίουσα κέντροις, <ἐὴ>, φοιταλέοις, ἐή.
σκιρτημάτων δὲ νήστισιν αἰκίαις 625 (600)
λαβρόσυτος ἦλθον, <Ἥρας>
ἐπικότοισι μήδεσι δαμεῖσα. δυσ-
δαιμόνων δὲ τίνες οἵ,
ἐή, οἵ ἐγὼ
μογοῦσιν; ἀλλά μοι τορῶς 630
τέκμηρον ὅ τι μ᾽ ἐπαμμένει (605)

παθεῖν, τί *μῆχαρ, ἢ τί φάρμακον νόσου·
δεῖξον, εἴπερ οἶσθα·
θρόει, φράζε τᾷ
δυσπλάνῳ παρθένῳ.   635

ΠΡ. λέξω τορῶς σοι πᾶν ὅπερ χρῄζεις μαθεῖν,
οὐκ ἐμπλέκων αἰνίγματ᾽, ἀλλ᾽ ἁπλῷ λόγῳ,   (610)
ὥσπερ δίκαιον πρὸς φίλους οἴγειν στόμα·
πυρὸς βροτοῖς δοτῆρ᾽ ὁρᾷς Προμηθέα.

ΙΩ. ὦ κοινὸν ὠφέλημα θνητοῖσιν φανείς,   640
τλῆμον Προμηθεῦ, τοῦ δίκην πάσχεις τάδε;

ΠΡ. ἁρμοῖ πέπαυμαι τοὺς ἐμοὺς θρηνῶν πόνους.   (615)

ΙΩ. οὔκουν πόροις ἂν τήνδε δωρειὰν ἐμοί;

ΠΡ. λέγ᾽ ἥντιν᾽ αἰτῇ· πᾶν γὰρ ἂν πύθοιό μου.

ΙΩ. σήμηνον ὅστις ἐν φάραγγί σ᾽ ὤχμασεν.   645

ΠΡ. βούλευμα μὲν τὸ Δῖον, Ἡφαίστου δὲ χείρ.

ΙΩ. ποίων δὲ ποινὰς ἀμπλακημάτων τίνεις;   (620)

ΠΡ. τοσοῦτον ἀρκῶ σοι σαφηνίσαι μόνον.

ΙΩ. καὶ πρός γε τούτοις τέρμα τῆς ἐμῆς πλάνης
δεῖξον, τίς ἔσται τῇ ταλαιπώρῳ χρόνος.   650

ΠΡ. τὸ μὴ μαθεῖν σοι κρεῖσσον ἢ μαθεῖν τάδε.

ΙΩ. μήτοι με κρύψῃς τοῦθ᾽ ὅπερ μέλλω παθεῖν.   (625)

ΠΡ. ἀλλ᾽ οὐ μεγαίρω τοῦδε τοῦ δωρήματος.

ΙΩ. τί δῆτα μέλλεις μὴ οὐ γεγωνίσκειν τὸ πᾶν;

ΠΡ. φθόνος μὲν οὐδείς, σὰς δ᾽ ὀκνῶ θρᾶξαι φρένας. 655

ΙΩ. μή μου προκήδου μᾶσσον ὡς ἐμοὶ γλυκύ.

ΠΡ. ἐπεὶ προθυμῇ, χρὴ λέγειν· ἄκουε δή.   (630)

ΧΟ. μήπω γε· μοῖραν δ᾽ ἡδονῆς κἀμοὶ πόρε.
τὴν τῆσδε πρῶτον ἱστορήσωμεν νόσον,
αὐτῆς λεγούσης τὰς πολυφθόρους τύχας·   660
τὰ λοιπὰ δ᾽ ἄθλων σοῦ διδαχθήτω πάρα.

ΠΡ. σὸν ἔργον, Ἰοῖ, ταῖσδ᾽ ὑπουργῆσαι χάριν,   (635)

ἄλλως τε πάντως καὶ κασιγνήταις πατρός.
ὡς τἀποκλαῦσαι κἀποδύρασθαι τύχας
ἐνταῦθ' ὅπου μέλλοι τις οἴσεσθαι δάκρυ   665
πρὸς τῶν κλυόντων, ἀξίαν τριβὴν ἔχει.

ΙΩ. οὐκ οἶδ' ὅπως ὑμῖν ἀπιστῆσαί με χρή,   (640)
σαφεῖ δὲ μύθῳ πᾶν ὅπερ προσχρήζετε
πεύσεσθε· καίτοι καὶ λέγουσ' ὀδύρομαι
θεόσσυτον χειμῶνα καὶ διαφθορὰν   670
μορφῆς, ὅθεν μοι σχετλίᾳ προσέπτατο.

αἰεὶ γὰρ ὄψεις ἔννυχοι πωλεύμεναι   (645)
ἐς παρθενῶνας τοὺς ἐμοὺς παρηγόρουν
λείοισι μύθοις "ὦ μέγ' εὔδαιμον κόρη,
τί παρθενεύῃ δαρόν, ἐξόν σοι γάμου   675
τυχεῖν μεγίστου; Ζεὺς γὰρ ἱμέρου βέλει
πρὸς σοῦ τέθαλπται καὶ συναίρεσθαι Κύπριν   (650)
θέλει· σὺ δ', ὦ παῖ, μὴ 'πολακτίσῃς λέχος
τὸ Ζηνός, ἀλλ' ἔξελθε πρὸς Λέρνης βαθὺν
λειμῶνα, ποίμνας βουστάσεις τε πρὸς πατρός, 680
ὡς ἂν τὸ Δῖον ὄμμα λωφήσῃ πόθου."
τοιοῖσδε πάσας εὐφρόνας ὀνείρασιν   (655)
ξυνειχόμην δύστηνος, ἔστε δὴ πατρὶ
ἔτλην γεγωνεῖν νυκτίφαντ' ὀνείρατα.
ὁ δ' ἔς τε Πυθὼ κἀπὶ Δωδώνης πυκνοὺς   685
θεοπρόπους ἴαλλεν, ὡς μάθοι τί χρὴ
δρῶντ' ἢ λέγοντα δαίμοσιν πράσσειν φίλα.   (660)
ἧκον δ' ἀναγγέλλοντες αἰολοστόμους
χρησμοὺς ἀσήμους δυσκρίτως τ' εἰρημένους.
τέλος δ' ἐναργὴς βάξις ἦλθεν Ἰνάχῳ   690
σαφῶς ἐπισκήπτουσα καὶ μυθουμένη
ἔξω δόμων τε καὶ πάτρας ὠθεῖν ἐμέ,   (665)
ἄφετον ἀλᾶσθαι γῆς ἐπ' ἐσχάτοις ὅροις·

κεἰ μὴ θέλοι, πυρωτὸν ἐκ Διὸς μολεῖν
κεραυνὸν, ὃς πᾶν ἐξαϊστώσει γένος. 695
τοιοῖσδε πεισθεὶς Λοξίου μαντεύμασιν
ἐξήλασέν με κἀπέκλῃσε δωμάτων, (670)
ἄκουσαν ἄκων· ἀλλ' ἐπηνάγκαζέ νιν
Διὸς χαλινὸς πρὸς βίαν πράσσειν τάδε.
εὐθὺς δὲ μορφὴ καὶ φρένες διάστροφοι 700
ἦσαν, κεραστὶς δ', ὡς ὁρᾶτ', ὀξυστόμῳ
μύωπι χρισθεῖσ' ἐμμανεῖ σκιρτήματι (675)
ᾖσσον πρὸς εὔποτόν τε Κερχνείας ῥέος
Λέρνης *τε κρήνην· βουκόλος δὲ γηγενὴς
ἄκρατος ὀργὴν Ἄργος ὡμάρτει, πυκνοῖς 705
ὅσσοις δεδορκὼς τοὺς ἐμοὺς κατὰ στίβους.
ἀπροσδόκητος δ' αὐτὸν ἀφνίδιος μόρος (680)
τοῦ ζῆν ἀπεστέρησεν. οἰστροπλὴξ δ' ἐγὼ
μάστιγι θείᾳ γῆν πρὸ γῆς ἐλαύνομαι.
κλύεις τὰ πραχθέντ'· εἰ δ' ἔχεις εἰπεῖν ὅ τι 710
λοιπὸν πόνων, σήμαινε· μηδέ μ' οἰκτίσας
σύνθαλπε μύθοις ψευδέσιν· νόσημα γὰρ (685)
αἴσχιστον εἶναί φημι συνθέτους λόγους.

ΧΟ. ἔα ἔα, ἄπεχε, φεῦ·
οὔποθ' <ὧδ'>, οὔποτ' ηὔχουν ξένους 715
μολεῖσθαι λόγους ἐς ἀκοὰν ἐμάν,
οὐδ' ὧδε δυσθέατα καὶ δύσοιστα, (690)
πήματα, λύματα, δείματ' ἀμφά-
κει κέντρῳ *ψύξειν ψυχὰν [ἐμάν].
ἰὼ ἰὼ μοῖρα μοῖρα, 720
πέφρικ' εἰσιδοῦσα πρᾶξιν Ἰοῦς. (695)

ΠΡ. πρῴ γε στενάζεις καὶ φόβου πλέα τις εἶ·
ἐπίσχες ἔστ' ἂν καὶ τὰ λοιπὰ προσμάθῃς.

ΧΟ. λέγ', ἐκδίδασκε· τοῖς νοσοῦσί τοι γλυκὺ
τὸ λοιπὸν ἄλγος προυξεπίστασθαι τορῶς.   725

ΠΡ. τὴν πρίν γε χρείαν ἠνύσασθ' ἐμοῦ πάρα   (700)
κούφως· μαθεῖν γὰρ τῆσδε πρῶτ' ἐχρῄζετε
τὸν ἀμφ' ἑαυτῆς ἄθλον ἐξηγουμένης·
τὰ λοιπὰ νῦν ἀκούσαθ', οἷα χρὴ πάθη
τλῆναι πρὸς Ἥρας τήνδε τὴν νεάνιδα.   730
σύ τ', Ἰνάχειον σπέρμα, τοὺς ἐμοὺς λόγους   (705)
θυμῷ βάλ', ὡς ἂν τέρματ' ἐκμάθῃς ὁδοῦ.
πρῶτον μὲν ἐνθένδ' ἡλίου πρὸς ἀντολὰς
στρέψασα σαυτὴν στεῖχ' ἀνηρότους γύας·
Σκύθας δ' ἀφίξῃ νομάδας, οἳ πλεκτὰς στέγας   735
πεδάρσιοι ναίουσ' ἐπ' εὐκύκλοις ὄχοις,   (710)
ἑκηβόλοις τόξοισιν ἐξηρτυμένοι·
οἷς μὴ πελάζειν, ἀλλ' ἁλιστόνοις *πόδας
χρίμπτουσα ῥαχίαισιν ἐκπερᾶν χθόνα.
λαιᾶς δὲ χειρὸς οἱ σιδηροτέκτονες   740
οἰκοῦσι Χάλυβες, οὓς φυλάξασθαί σε χρή·   (715)
ἀνήμεροι γὰρ οὐδὲ πρόσπλατοι ξένοις.
ἥξεις δ' Ὑβρίστην ποταμὸν οὐ ψευδώνυμον,
ὃν μὴ περάσῃς, οὐ γὰρ εὔβατος περᾶν,
πρὶν ἂν πρὸς αὐτὸν Καύκασον μόλῃς, ὀρῶν   745
ὕψιστον, ἔνθα ποταμὸς ἐκφυσᾷ μένος   (720)
κροτάφων ἀπ' αὐτῶν. ἀστρογείτονας δὲ χρὴ
κορυφὰς *ὑπερβαλοῦσαν ἐς μεσημβρινὴν
βῆναι κέλευθον, ἔνθ' Ἀμαζόνων στρατὸν
ἥξεις στυγάνορ', αἳ Θεμίσκυράν ποτε   750
κατοικιοῦσιν ἀμφὶ Θερμώδονθ', ἵνα   (725)
τραχεῖα πόντου Σαλμυδησσία γνάθος
ἐχθρόξενος ναύταισι, μητρυιὰ νεῶν·
αὗταί σ' ὁδηγήσουσι καὶ μάλ' ἀσμένως.

ἰσθμὸν δ' ἐπ' αὐταῖς στενοπόροις λίμνης πύλαις 755
Κιμμερικὸν ἥξεις, ὃν θρασυσπλάγχνως σε χρὴ (730)
λιποῦσαν αὐλῶν' ἐκπερᾶν Μαιωτικόν·
ἔσται δὲ θνητοῖς εἰσαεὶ λόγος μέγας
τῆς σῆς πορείας, Βόσπορος δ' ἐπώνυμος
κεκλήσεται. λιποῦσα δ' Εὐρώπης πέδον   760
ἤπειρον ἥξεις Ἀσιάδ'. ἆρ' ὑμῖν δοκεῖ   (735)
ὁ τῶν θεῶν τύραννος ἐς τὰ πάνθ' ὁμῶς
βίαιος εἶναι; τῇδε γὰρ θνητῇ θεὸς
χρήζων μιγῆναι τάσδ' ἐπέρριψεν πλάνας.
πικροῦ δ' ἔκυρσας, ὦ κόρη, τῶν σῶν γάμων 765
μνηστῆρος. οὓς γὰρ νῦν ἀκήκοας λόγους,   (740)
εἶναι δόκει σοὶ μηδέπω 'ν προοιμίοις.
ΙΩ.   ἰώ μοί μοι, ἐή.
ΠΡ.   σὺ δ' αὖ κέκραγας κἀναμυχθίζῃ· τί που
δράσεις, ὅταν τὰ λοιπὰ πυνθάνῃ κακά;   770
ΧΟ.   ἦ γάρ τι λοιπὸν τῇδε πημάτων ἐρεῖς;   (745)
ΠΡ.   δυσχείμερόν γε πέλαγος ἀτηρᾶς δύης.
ΙΩ.   τί δῆτ' ἐμοὶ ζῆν κέρδος, ἀλλ' οὐκ ἐν τάχει
ἔρριψ' ἐμαυτὴν τῆσδ' ἀπὸ στύφλου πέτρας,
ὅπως πέδοι σκήψασα τῶν πάντων πόνων   775
ἀπηλλάγην; κρεῖσσον γὰρ εἰσάπαξ θανεῖν   (750)
ἢ τὰς ἁπάσας ἡμέρας πάσχειν κακῶς.
ΠΡ.   ἦ δυσπετῶς ἂν τοὺς ἐμοὺς ἄθλους φέροις,
ὅτῳ θανεῖν μέν ἐστιν οὐ πεπρωμένον·
αὕτη γὰρ ἦν ἂν πημάτων ἀπαλλαγή·   780
νῦν δ' οὐδέν ἐστι τέρμα μοι προκείμενον   (755)
μόχθων, πρὶν ἂν Ζεὺς ἐκπέσῃ τυραννίδος.
ΙΩ.   ἦ γάρ ποτ' ἔστιν ἐκπεσεῖν ἀρχῆς Δία;
ΠΡ.   ἥδοι' ἄν, οἶμαι, τήνδ' ἰδοῦσα συμφοράν.
ΙΩ.   πῶς δ' οὐκ ἄν, ἥτις ἐκ Διὸς πάσχω κακῶς; 785

ΠΡ. ὡς τοίνυν ὄντων τῶνδε μανθάνειν πάρα. (760)
ΙΩ. πρὸς τοῦ τύραννα σκῆπτρα συληθήσεται;
ΠΡ. πρὸς αὐτὸς αὑτοῦ κενοφρόνων βουλευμάτων.
ΙΩ. ποίῳ τρόπῳ; σήμηνον, εἰ μή τις βλάβη.
ΠΡ. γαμεῖ γάμον τοιοῦτον ᾧ ποτ' ἀσχαλᾷ. 790
ΙΩ. θέορτον, ἢ βρότειον; εἰ ῥητὸν, φράσον. (765)
ΠΡ. τί δ' ὄντιν'; οὐ γὰρ ῥητὸν αὐδᾶσθαι τόδε.
ΙΩ. ἦ πρὸς δάμαρτος ἐξανίσταται θρόνων;
ΠΡ. ἢ τέξεταί γε παῖδα φέρτερον πατρός.
ΙΩ. οὐδ' ἔστιν αὐτῷ τῆσδ' ἀποστροφὴ τύχης; 795
ΠΡ. οὐ δῆτα, πλὴν ἔγωγ' ἂν ἐκ δεσμῶν λυθείς. (770)
ΙΩ. τίς οὖν ὁ λύσων ἐστὶν ἄκοντος Διός;
ΠΡ. τῶν σῶν τιν' αὐτῶν ἐκγόνων εἶναι χρεών.
ΙΩ. πῶς εἶπας; ἦ 'μὸς παῖς σ' ἀπαλλάξει κακῶν;
ΠΡ. τρίτος γε γένναν πρὸς δέκ' ἄλλαισιν γοναῖς. 800
ΙΩ. ἥδ' οὐκέτ' εὐξύμβλητος ἡ χρησμῳδία. (775)
ΠΡ. καὶ μηδὲ σαυτῆς γ' ἐκμαθεῖν ζήτει πόνους.
ΙΩ. μή μοι προτείνων κέρδος, εἶτ' ἀποστέρει.
ΠΡ. δυοῖν λόγοιν σε θατέρῳ δωρήσομαι.
ΙΩ. ποίοιν; πρόδειξον αἵρεσίν τ' ἐμοὶ δίδου. 805
ΠΡ. δίδωμ'· ἑλοῦ γάρ· ἢ πόνων τὰ λοιπά σοι (780)
    φράσω σαφηνῶς, ἢ τὸν ἐκλύσοντ' ἐμέ.
ΧΟ. τούτοιν σὺ τὴν μὲν τῇδε, τὴν δ' ἐμοὶ χάριν
    θέσθαι θέλησον, μηδ' ἀτιμάσῃς *λόγου·
    καὶ τῇδε μὲν γέγωνε τὴν λοιπὴν πλάνην, 810
    ἐμοὶ δὲ τὸν λύσοντα· τοῦτο γὰρ ποθῶ. (785)
ΠΡ. ἐπεὶ προθυμεῖσθ', οὐκ ἐναντιώσομαι
    τὸ μὴ οὐ γεγωνεῖν πᾶν ὅσον προσχρῄζετε.
    σοὶ πρῶτον, Ἰοῖ, πολύδονον πλάνην φράσω,
    ἣν ἐγγράφου σὺ μνήμοσιν δέλτοις φρενῶν. 815
    ὅταν περάσῃς ῥεῖθρον ἠπείροιν ὅρον, (790)

πρὸς ἀντολὰς φλογῶπας ἡλιοστιβεῖς
*   *   *   *   *   *   *
πόντου περῶσα φλοῖσβον, ἔστ' ἂν ἐξίκῃ
πρὸς Γοργόνεια πεδία Κισθήνης, ἵνα
αἱ Φορκίδες ναίουσι δηναιαὶ κόραι 820
τρεῖς κυκνόμορφοι, κοινὸν ὄμμ' ἐκτημέναι, (795)
μονόδοντες, ἃς οὔθ' ἥλιος προσδέρκεται
ἀκτῖσιν οὔθ' ἡ νύκτερος μήνη ποτέ.
πέλας δ' ἀδελφαὶ τῶνδε τρεῖς κατάπτεροι,
δρακοντόμαλλοι Γοργόνες βροτοστυγεῖς, 825
ἃς θνητὸς οὐδεὶς εἰσιδὼν ἕξει πνοάς. (800)
τοιοῦτο μέν σοι τοῦτο φρούριον λέγω·
ἄλλην δ' ἄκουσον δυσχερῆ θεωρίαν.
ὀξυστόμους γὰρ Ζηνὸς ἀκραγεῖς κύνας
γρῦπας φύλαξαι, τόν τε μουνῶπα στρατὸν 830
Ἀριμασπὸν ἱπποβάμον' οἳ χρυσόρρυτον (805)
οἰκοῦσιν ἀμφὶ νᾶμα Πλούτωνος πόρου·
τούτοις σὺ μὴ πέλαζε. τηλουρὸν δὲ *γῆς
ἥξεις κελαινὸν φῦλον, οἳ πρὸς ἡλίου
ναίουσι πηγαῖς, ἔνθα ποταμὸς Αἰθίοψ. 835
τούτου παρ' ὄχθας ἕρφ', ἕως ἂν ἐξίκῃ (810)
καταβασμὸν, ἔνθα Βιβλίνων ὀρῶν ἄπο
ἵησι σεπτὸν Νεῖλος εὔποτον ῥέος.
οὗτός σ' ὁδώσει τὴν τρίγωνον ἐς χθόνα
Νειλῶτιν, οὗ δὴ τὴν μακρὰν ἀποικίαν, 840
Ἰοῖ, πέπρωται σοί τε καὶ τέκνοις κτίσαι.
τῶνδ' εἴ τί σοι ψελλόν τε καὶ δυσεύρετον, (815)
ἐπανδίπλαζε καὶ σαφῶς ἐκμάνθανε·
σχολὴ δὲ πλείων ἢ θέλω πάρεστί μοι.

ΧΟ. εἰ μέν τι τῇδε λοιπὸν ἢ παρειμένον 845
ἔχεις γεγωνεῖν τῆς πολυφθόρου πλάνης, (820)

λέγ'· εἰ δὲ πάντ' εἴρηκας, ἡμῖν αὖ χάριν
δὸς ἥνπερ αἰτούμεσθα, μέμνησαι δέ που.

ΠΡ. τὸ πᾶν πορείας ἥδε τέρμ' ἀκήκοεν·
ὅπως δ' ἂν εἰδῇ, μὴ μάτην κλύουσά μου,   850
ἃ πρὶν μολεῖν δεῦρ' ἐκμεμόχθηκεν φράσω,   (825)
τεκμήριον τοῦτ' αὐτὸ δοὺς μύθων ἐμῶν.
ὄχλον μὲν οὖν τὸν πλεῖστον ἐκλείψω λόγων,
πρὸς αὐτὸ δ' εἶμι τέρμα σῶν πλανημάτων.
ἐπεὶ γὰρ ἦλθες πρὸς Μολοσσὰ γάπεδα,   855
τὴν αἰπύνωτόν τ' ἀμφὶ Δωδώνην, ἵνα   (830)
μαντεῖα θᾶκός τ' ἐστὶ Θεσπρωτοῦ Διός,
τέρας τ' ἄπιστον, αἱ προσήγοροι δρύες,
ὑφ' ὧν σὺ λαμπρῶς κοὐδὲν αἰνικτηρίως
προσηγορεύθης ἡ Διὸς κλεινὴ δάμαρ   860
μέλλουσ' ἔσεσθαι·—τῶνδε προσσαίνει σέ τι;—   (835)
ἐντεῦθεν οἰστρήσασα τὴν παρακτίαν
κέλευθον ᾖξας πρὸς μέγαν κόλπον Ῥέας,
ἀφ' οὗ παλιμπλάγκτοισι χειμάζῃ δρόμοις·
χρόνον δὲ τὸν μέλλοντα πόντιος μυχός,   865
σαφῶς ἐπίστασ', Ἰόνιος κεκλήσεται,   (840)
τῆς σῆς πορείας μνῆμα τοῖς πᾶσιν βροτοῖς.
σημεῖά σοι τάδ' ἐστὶ τῆς ἐμῆς φρενός,
ὡς δέρκεται πλέον τι τοῦ πεφασμένου.
τὰ λοιπὰ δ' ὑμῖν τῇδέ τ' ἐς κοινὸν φράσω,   870
ἐς ταὐτὸν ἐλθὼν τῶν πάλαι λόγων ἴχνος.   (845)
ἔστιν πόλις Κάνωβος ἐσχάτη χθονός,
Νείλου πρὸς αὐτῷ στόματι καὶ προσχώματι·
ἐνταῦθα δή σε Ζεὺς τίθησιν ἔμφρονα
ἐπαφῶν ἀταρβεῖ χειρὶ καὶ θιγὼν μόνον.   875
ἐπώνυμον δὲ τῶν Διὸς γεννημάτων   (850)
τέξεις κελαινὸν Ἔπαφον, ὃς καρπώσεται

ὅσην πλατύρρους Νεῖλος ἀρδεύει χθόνα·
πέμπτη δ' ἀπ' αὐτοῦ γέννα πεντηκοντάπαις
πάλιν πρὸς Ἄργος οὐχ ἑκοῦσ' ἐλεύσεται   880
θηλύσπορος, φεύγουσα συγγενῆ γάμον   (855)
ἀνεψιῶν· οἱ δ' ἐπτοημένοι φρένας,
κίρκοι πελειῶν οὐ μακρὰν λελειμμένοι,
ἥξουσι θηρεύοντες οὐ θηρασίμους
γάμους, φθόνον δὲ σωμάτων ἕξει θεός·   885
Πελασγία δὲ δέξεται, θηλυκτόνῳ   (860)
Ἄρει δαμέντων νυκτιφρουρήτῳ θράσει.
γυνὴ γὰρ ἄνδρ' ἕκαστον αἰῶνος στερεῖ,
δίθηκτον ἐν σφαγαῖσι βάψασα ξίφος·
τοιάδ' ἐς ἐχθροὺς τοὺς ἐμοὺς ἔλθοι Κύπρις.   890
μίαν δὲ παίδων ἵμερος θέλξει τὸ μὴ   (865)
κτεῖναι σύνευνον, ἀλλ' ἀπαμβλυνθήσεται
γνώμην· δυοῖν δὲ θάτερον βουλήσεται,
κλύειν ἄναλκις μᾶλλον ἢ μιαιφόνος·
αὕτη κατ' Ἄργος βασιλικὸν τέξει γένος.   895
μακροῦ λόγου δεῖ ταῦτ' ἐπεξελθεῖν τορῶς.   (870)
*σπόρος γε μὴν ἐκ τῆσδε φύσεται θρασύς,
τόξοισι κλεινός, ὃς πόνων ἐκ τῶνδ' ἐμὲ
λύσει. τοιόνδε χρησμὸν ἡ παλαιγενὴς
μήτηρ ἐμοὶ διῆλθε Τιτανὶς Θέμις·   900
ὅπως δὲ χὤπῃ, ταῦτα δεῖ μακροῦ λόγου   (875)
εἰπεῖν, σύ τ' οὐδὲν ἐκμαθοῦσα κερδανεῖς.

ΙΩ.   ἐλελεῦ, ἐλελεῦ,
ὑπό μ' αὖ σφάκελος καὶ φρενοπλῆγες
μανίαι θάλπουσ', οἴστρου δ' ἄρδις   905
χρίει μ' ἄπυρος·   (880)
κραδία δὲ φόβῳ φρένα λακτίζει.

τροχοδινεῖται δ' ὄμμαθ' ἐλίγδην,
ἔξω δὲ δρόμου φέρομαι λύσσης
πνεύματι μάργῳ, γλώσσης ἀκρατής·   910
θολεροὶ δὲ λόγοι παίουσ' εἰκῇ   (885)
στυγνῆς πρὸς κύμασιν ἄτης.   [Exit.

[Τρίτον Στάσιμον.]

ΧΟ. Ἦ σοφὸς ἦ σοφὸς [ἦν] ὃς   [Στρ.
πρῶτος ἐν γνώμᾳ τόδ' ἐβάστασε καὶ γλώσ-
σᾳ διεμυθολόγησεν,   915
ὡς τὸ κηδεῦσαι καθ' ἑαυ-
τὸν ἀριστεύει μακρῷ,   (890)
καὶ μήτε τῶν πλού-
τῳ διαθρυπτομένων
μήτε τῶν γέννᾳ μεγαλυνομένων   920
ὄντα χερνήταν ἐραστεῦσαι γάμων.

μήποτε μήποτέ μ', ὦ   ['Αντ.
<πότνιαι> Μοῖραι, λεχέων Διὸς εὐνά-   (895)
τειραν ἴδοισθε πέλουσαν·
μηδὲ πλαθείην γαμέτᾳ   925
τινὶ τῶν ἐξ οὐρανοῦ.
ταρβῶ γὰρ ἀστερ-
γάνορα παρθενίαν
εἰσορῶσ' Ἰοῦς *ἀμαλαπτομέναν
δυσπλάνοις Ἥρας ἀλατείαις πόνων.   930 (900)

ἐμοὶ *δέ γ', ὅτε μὲν ὁμαλὸς ὁ γάμος,   ['Επῳδ.
ἄφοβος, *οὐδὲ δέδια· μηδὲ κρεισσό-
νων θεῶν [ἔρως] ἄφυ-
κτον ὄμμα προσδράκοι με.
ἀπόλεμος ὅδε γ' ὁ πόλεμος, ἄπορα   935

πόριμος· οὐδ' ἔχω τίς ἂν γενοίμαν·
τὰν Διὸς γὰρ οὐχ ὁρῶ
μῆτιν ὅπᾳ φύγοιμ' ἄν.

[Ἔξοδος.]

ΠΡ. Ἦ μὴν ἔτι Ζεύς, καίπερ αὐθάδη φρονῶν,   (905)
ἔσται ταπεινός, οἷον ἐξαρτύεται   940
γάμον γαμεῖν, ὃς αὐτὸν ἐκ τυραννίδος
θρόνων τ' ἄιστον ἐκβαλεῖ· πατρὸς δ' ἀρὰ   (910)
Κρόνου τότ' ἤδη παντελῶς κρανθήσεται,
ἣν ἐκπίτνων ἠρᾶτο δηναιῶν θρόνων.
τοιῶνδε μόχθων ἐκτροπὴν οὐδεὶς θεῶν   945
δύναιτ' ἂν αὐτῷ πλὴν ἐμοῦ δεῖξαι σαφῶς.
ἐγὼ τάδ' οἶδα χῷ τρόπῳ. πρὸς ταῦτά νυν   (915)
θαρσῶν καθήσθω τοῖς πεδαρσίοις κτύποις
πιστὸς τινάσσων τ' ἐν χεροῖν πύρπνουν βέλος.
οὐδὲν γὰρ αὐτῷ ταῦτ' ἐπαρκέσει τὸ μὴ οὐ   950
πεσεῖν ἀτίμως πτώματ' οὐκ ἀνασχετά·
τοῖον παλαιστὴν νῦν παρασκευάζεται   (920)
ἐπ' αὐτὸς αὑτῷ, δυσμαχώτατον τέρας·
ὃς δὴ κεραυνοῦ κρείσσον' εὑρήσει φλόγα,
βροντῆς θ' ὑπερβάλλοντα καρτερὸν κτύπον· 955
θαλασσίαν τε γῆς τινάκτειραν νόσον,
τρίαιναν, αἰχμὴν τὴν Ποσειδῶνος, σκεδᾷ.   (925)
πταίσας δὲ τῷδε πρὸς κακῷ μαθήσεται
ὅσον τό τ' ἄρχειν καὶ τὸ δουλεύειν δίχα.

ΧΟ. σύ θην ἃ χρῄζεις, ταῦτ' ἐπιγλωσσᾷ Διός.   960
ΠΡ. ἅπερ τελεῖται, πρὸς δ' ἃ βούλομαι λέγω.
ΧΟ. καὶ προσδοκᾶν χρὴ δεσπόσειν Ζηνός τινα;   (930)
ΠΡ. καὶ τῶνδέ γ' ἕξει δυσλοφωτέρους πόνους.
ΧΟ. πῶς δ' οὐχὶ ταρβεῖς τοιάδ' ἐκρίπτων ἔπη;

ΠΡ. τί δ' ἂν φοβοίμην ᾧ θανεῖν οὐ μόρσιμον; 965
ΧΟ. ἀλλ' ἆθλον ἄν σοι τοῦδ' ἔτ' ἀλγίω πόροι.
ΠΡ. ὁ δ' οὖν ποιείτω· πάντα προσδόκητά μοι. (935)
ΧΟ. οἱ προσκυνοῦντες τὴν Ἀδράστειαν σοφοί.
ΠΡ. σέβου, προσεύχου, θῶπτε τὸν κρατοῦντ' ἀεί.
ἐμοὶ δ' ἔλασσον Ζηνὸς ἢ μηδὲν μέλει. 970
δράτω, κρατείτω τόνδε τὸν βραχὺν χρόνον
ὅπως θέλει· δαρὸν γὰρ οὐκ ἄρξει θεοῖς. (940)

[*Enter* HERMES.]

ἀλλ' εἰσορῶ γὰρ τόνδε τὸν Διὸς τρόχιν,
τὸν τοῦ τυράννου τοῦ νέου διάκονον·
πάντως τι καινὸν ἀγγελῶν ἐλήλυθεν. 975
ΕΡ. σὲ τὸν σοφιστήν, τὸν πικρῶς ὑπέρπικρον,
τὸν ἐξαμαρτόντ' ἐς θεοὺς ἐφημέροις (945)
πορόντα τιμάς, τὸν πυρὸς κλέπτην λέγω·
πατὴρ ἄνωγέ σ' οὕστινας κομπεῖς γάμους
αὐδᾶν, πρὸς ὧν τ' ἐκεῖνος ἐκπίπτει κράτους· 980
καὶ ταῦτα μέντοι μηδὲν αἰνικτηρίως,
ἀλλ' αὔθ' ἕκαστ' ἔκφραζε· μηδέ μοι διπλᾶς (950)
ὁδούς, Προμηθεῦ, προσβάλῃς· ὁρᾷς δ' ὅτι
Ζεὺς τοῖς τοιούτοις οὐχὶ μαλθακίζεται.
ΠΡ. σεμνόστομός γε καὶ φρονήματος πλέως 985
ὁ μῦθός ἐστιν, ὡς θεῶν ὑπηρέτου.
νέον νέοι κρατεῖτε καὶ δοκεῖτε δὴ (955)
ναίειν ἀπενθῆ πέργαμ'· οὐκ ἐκ τῶνδ' ἐγὼ
δισσοὺς τυράννους ἐκπεσόντας ἠσθόμην;
τρίτον δὲ τὸν νῦν κοιρανοῦντ' ἐπόψομαι 990
αἴσχιστα καὶ τάχιστα. μὴ τί σοι δοκῶ
ταρβεῖν ὑποπτήσσειν τε τοὺς νέους θεούς; (960)
πολλοῦ γε καὶ τοῦ παντὸς ἐλλείπω. σὺ δὲ

κέλευθον ἥνπερ ἦλθες ἐγκόνει πάλιν·
πεύσει γὰρ οὐδὲν ὧν ἀνιστορεῖς ἐμέ.   995

ΕΡ. τοιοῖσδε μέντοι καὶ πρὶν αὐθαδίσμασιν
ἐς τάσδε σαυτὸν πημονὰς *κατούρισας.   (965)

ΠΡ. τῆς σῆς λατρείας τὴν ἐμὴν δυσπραξίαν,
σαφῶς ἐπίστασ', οὐκ ἂν ἀλλάξαιμ' ἐγώ.

ΕΡ. κρεῖσσον γὰρ οἶμαι τῆδε λατρεύειν πέτρᾳ   1000
ἢ πατρὶ φῦναι Ζηνὶ πιστὸν ἄγγελον.

ΠΡ. οὕτως ὑβρίζειν τοὺς ὑβρίζοντας χρεών.   (970)

ΕΡ. χλιδᾶν ἔοικας τοῖς παροῦσι πράγμασιν.

ΠΡ. χλιδῶ; χλιδῶντας ὧδε τοὺς ἐμοὺς ἐγὼ
ἐχθροὺς ἴδοιμι· καὶ σὲ δ' ἐν τούτοις λέγω.   1005

ΕΡ. ἦ κἀμὲ γάρ τι συμφορᾶς ἐπαιτιᾷ;

ΠΡ. ἁπλῷ λόγῳ τοὺς πάντας ἐχθαίρω θεούς,   (975)
ὅσοι παθόντες εὖ κακοῦσί μ' ἐκδίκως.

ΕΡ. κλύω σ' ἐγὼ μεμηνότ' οὐ σμικρὰν νόσον.

ΠΡ. νοσοῖμ' ἄν, εἰ νόσημα τοὺς ἐχθροὺς στυγεῖν.   1010

ΕΡ. εἴης φορητὸς οὐκ ἄν, εἰ πράσσοις καλῶς.

ΠΡ. ὤμοι.

ΕΡ.   τόδε Ζεὺς τοὔπος οὐκ ἐπίσταται.   (980)

ΠΡ. ἀλλ' ἐκδιδάσκει πάνθ' ὁ γηράσκων χρόνος.

ΕΡ. καὶ μὴν σύ γ' οὔπω σωφρονεῖν ἐπίστασαι.

ΠΡ. σὲ γὰρ προσηύδων οὐκ ἂν ὄνθ' ὑπηρέτην.   1015

ΕΡ. ἐρεῖν ἔοικας οὐδὲν ὧν χρῄζει πατήρ.

ΠΡ. καὶ μὴν ὀφείλων γ' ἂν τίνοιμ' αὐτῷ χάριν.   (985)

ΕΡ. ἐκερτόμησας δῆθεν *ὥστε παῖδά με.

ΠΡ. οὐ γὰρ σὺ παῖς τε κἄτι τοῦδ' ἀνούστερος,
εἰ προσδοκᾷς ἐμοῦ τι πεύσεσθαι πάρα;   1020
οὐκ ἔστιν αἴκισμ' οὐδὲ μηχάνημ' ὅτῳ
προτρέψεταί με Ζεὺς γεγωνῆσαι τάδε,   (990)
πρὶν ἂν χαλασθῇ δεσμὰ λυμαντήρια.

πρὸς ταῦτα ῥιπτέσθω μὲν αἰθαλοῦσσα φλόξ,
λευκοπτέρῳ δὲ νιφάδι καὶ βροντήμασιν   1025
χθονίοις κυκάτω πάντα καὶ ταρασσέτω·
γνάψει γὰρ οὐδὲν τῶνδέ μ' ὥστε καὶ φράσαι   (995)
πρὸς οὗ χρεών νιν ἐκπεσεῖν τυραννίδος.

ΕΡ. ὅρα νυν εἴ σοι ταῦτ' ἀρωγὰ φαίνεται.

ΠΡ. ὦπται πάλαι δὴ καὶ βεβούλευται τάδε.   1030

ΕΡ. τόλμησον, ὦ μάταιε, τόλμησόν ποτε
πρὸς τὰς παρούσας πημονὰς ὀρθῶς φρονεῖν.   (1000)

ΠΡ. ὀχλεῖς μάτην με κῦμ' ὅπως παρηγορῶν.
εἰσελθέτω σε μήποθ' ὡς ἐγὼ Διὸς
γνώμην φοβηθεὶς θηλύνους γενήσομαι   1035
καὶ λιπαρήσω τὸν μέγα στυγούμενον
γυναικομίμοις ὑπτιάσμασιν χερῶν   (1005)
λῦσαί με δεσμῶν τῶνδε· τοῦ παντὸς δέω.

ΕΡ. λέγων ἔοικα πολλὰ καὶ μάτην ἐρεῖν·
τέγγῃ γὰρ οὐδὲν οὐδὲ μαλθάσσῃ λιταῖς   1040
ἐμαῖς· δάκνων δὲ στόμιον ὡς νεοζυγὴς
πῶλος βιάζῃ καὶ πρὸς ἡνίας μάχῃ.   (1010)
ἀτὰρ σφοδρύνῃ γ' ἀσθενεῖ σοφίσματι.
αὐθαδία γὰρ τῷ φρονοῦντι μὴ καλῶς   1045
αὐτὴ καθ' αὑτὴν οὐδενὸς μεῖζον σθένει.

σκέψαι δ', ἐὰν μὴ τοῖς ἐμοῖς πεισθῇς λόγοις,
οἷός σε χειμὼν καὶ κακῶν τρικυμία   (1015)
ἔπεισ' ἄφυκτος· πρῶτα μὲν γὰρ ὀκρίδα
φάραγγα βροντῇ καὶ κεραυνίᾳ φλογὶ   1050
πατὴρ σπαράξει τήνδε, καὶ κρύψει δέμας
τὸ σόν, πετραία δ' ἀγκάλη σε βαστάσει.
μακρὸν δὲ μῆκος ἐκτελευτήσας χρόνου   (1020)
ἄψορρον ἥξεις ἐς φάος· Διὸς δέ τοι
πτηνὸς κύων, δαφοινὸς ἀετός, λάβρως

διαρταμήσει σώματος μέγα ῥάκος,   1055
ἄκλητος ἕρπων δαιταλεὺς πανήμερος,
κελαινόβρωτον δ' ἧπαρ ἐκθοινάσεται.   (1025)
τοιοῦδε μόχθου τέρμα μή τι προσδόκα,
πρὶν ἂν θεῶν τις διάδοχος τῶν σῶν πόνων
φανῇ, θελήσῃ τ' εἰς ἀναύγητον μολεῖν   1060
"Αιδην κνεφαῖά τ' ἀμφὶ Ταρτάρου βάθη.
πρὸς ταῦτα βούλευ'· ὡς ὅδ' οὐ πεπλασμένος (1030)
ὁ κόμπος, ἀλλὰ καὶ λίαν †εἰρημένος·
ψευδηγορεῖν γὰρ οὐκ ἐπίσταται στόμα
τὸ Δῖον, ἀλλὰ πᾶν ἔπος τελεῖ. σὺ δὲ   1065
πάπταινε καὶ φρόντιζε, μηδ' αὐθαδίαν
εὐβουλίας ἄμεινον ἡγήσῃ ποτέ.   (1035)

ΧΟ. ἡμῖν μὲν Ἑρμῆς οὐκ ἄκαιρα φαίνεται
λέγειν· ἄνωγε γάρ σε τὴν αὐθαδίαν
μεθέντ' ἐρευνᾶν τὴν σοφὴν εὐβουλίαν.
πιθοῦ· σοφῷ γὰρ αἰσχρὸν ἐξαμαρτάνειν.   1070

ΠΡ. εἰδότι τοί μοι τάσδ' ἀγγελίας   (1040)
ὅδ' ἐθώυξεν, πάσχειν δὲ κακῶς
ἐχθρὸν ὑπ' ἐχθρῶν οὐδὲν ἀεικές.
πρὸς ταῦτ' ἐπ' ἐμοὶ ῥιπτέσθω μὲν   1075
πυρὸς ἀμφήκης βόστρυχος, αἰθὴρ δ'
ἐρεθιζέσθω βροντῇ σφακέλῳ τ'   (1045)
ἀγρίων ἀνέμων· χθόνα δ' ἐκ πυθμένων
αὐταῖς ῥίζαις πνεῦμα κραδαίνοι,
κῦμα δὲ πόντου τραχεῖ ῥοθίῳ   1080
συγχώσειεν
τῶν τ' οὐρανίων ἄστρων διόδους·
ἔς τε κελαινὸν Τάρταρον ἄρδην   (1050)
ῥίψειε δέμας τοὐμὸν ἀνάγκης

5—2

στερραῖς δίναις·   1085
πάντως ἐμέ γ' οὐ θανατώσει.

ΕΡ. τοιάδε μέντοι τῶν φρενοπλήκτων
βουλεύματ' ἔπη τ' ἔστιν ἀκοῦσαι.   (1055)
τί γὰρ ἐλλείπει μὴ <οὐ> παραπαίειν
ἡ τοῦδ' *εὐχή; τί χαλᾷ μανιῶν;   1090
ἀλλ' οὖν ὑμεῖς γ' αἱ πημοσύναις
συγκάμνουσαι ταῖς τοῦδε τόπων
μετά ποι χωρεῖτ' ἐκ τῶνδε θοῶς,   (1060)
μὴ φρένας ὑμῶν ἠλιθιώσῃ
βροντῆς μύκημ' ἀτέραμνον.   1095

ΧΟ. ἄλλο τι φώνει καὶ παραμυθοῦ μ'
ὅ τι καὶ πείσεις· οὐ γὰρ δή που
τοῦτό γε τλητὸν παρέσυρας ἔπος.   (1065)
πῶς με κελεύεις κακότητ' ἀσκεῖν;
μετὰ τοῦδ' ὅ τι χρὴ πάσχειν ἐθέλω·   1100
τοὺς προδότας γὰρ μισεῖν ἔμαθον,
κοὐκ ἔστι νόσος
τῆσδ' ἥντιν' ἀπέπτυσα μᾶλλον.   (1070)

ΕΡ. ἀλλ' οὖν μέμνησθ' ἁγὼ προλέγω
μηδὲ πρὸς ἄτης θηραθεῖσαι   1105
μέμψησθε τύχην,
μηδέ ποτ' εἴπηθ' ὡς Ζεὺς ὑμᾶς
εἰς ἀπρόοπτον πῆμ' εἰσέβαλεν·
μὴ δῆτ', αὐταὶ δ' ὑμᾶς αὐτάς.   (1075)
εἰδυῖαι γὰρ κοὐκ ἐξαίφνης   1110
οὐδὲ λαθραίως
εἰς ἀπέραντον δίκτυον ἄτης
ἐμπλεχθήσεσθ' ὑπ' ἀνοίας.   [Exit.

ΠΡ. καὶ μὴν ἔργῳ κοὐκέτι μύθῳ   (1080)
χθὼν σεσάλευται·   1115

βρυχία δ' ἠχὼ παραμυκᾶται
βροντῆς, ἕλικες δ' ἐκλάμπουσι
στεροπῆς ζάπυροι, στρόμβοι δὲ κόνιν
εἰλίσσουσι· σκιρτᾷ δ' ἀνέμων   (1085)
πνεύματα πάντων εἰς ἄλληλα   1120
στάσιν ἀντίπνουν ἀποδεικνύμενα·
ξυντετάρακται δ' αἰθὴρ πόντῳ.
τοιάδ' ἐπ' ἐμοὶ ῥιπὴ Διόθεν
τεύχουσα φόβον στείχει φανερῶς.   (1090)
ὦ μητρὸς ἐμῆς σέβας, ὦ πάντων   1125
αἰθὴρ κοινὸν φάος εἰλίσσων,
ἐσορᾷς μ' ὡς ἔκδικα πάσχω.

[*The rock with* PROMETHEUS *chained to it, and the* CHORUS
grouped round him, sink out of sight.]

EXPLANATORY NOTES.

[*The other Attic dramatists are quoted from Dindorf's Poetae Scenici,*
1868 ; *the other plays of Aeschylus from Wecklein's edition,* 1885,
with Dindorf's numbering added in brackets. G. *stands for Goodwin's Greek Grammar,* 1895, M. *and* T. *for his Moods and Tenses,*
1889, *both referred to by sections; LS. for Liddell and Scott.*]

1. χθονὸς...τηλουρὸν...πέδον, *the farthest confines of the earth.*
χθονός partitive gen. with the local adj. as with adverbs like ποῦ,
πόρρω, &c. ; cf. 833 n., and 872 ἐσχάτη χθονός. (Edd. take χθονός
directly with πέδον as a poetic periphrasis for χθόνα, cf. 760, Sept. 291
(304) ποῖον...γαίας πέδον). τηλουρόν, probably from τῆλε and οὖρος =
ὅρος, though Wecklein derives it directly from (τηλός), cf. πον-ηρός,
οἰζ-υρός, &c.

2. Σκύθην for Σκυθικόν, as in 433, cf. Ag. 1253 (1254) "Ελλην'
ἐπίσταμαι φάτιν, Marsus aper (Hor.), the epithet personifying the non-
personal noun as in phrases like 787 τύραννα σκῆπτρα, παρθένος χείρ
(Eur.).

οἶμον perhaps hints at the nomadic habits of the Scythians, v. 735.
The Scythian track, the untrodden solitude is an oxymoron. [Οἶμος is
used for a *stripe* of inlaid metal on a breastplate in Il. 11. 24, but that
hardly justifies the translation *tract* here.]

3. "Ηφαιστε, σοὶ δέ: this order is common in poetry; cf. Soph.
O. C. 332 τέκνον, τί δ᾽ ἦλθες; also Il. 6. 429 "Εκτορ, ἀτὰρ σύ μοί ἐσσι
πατήρ. The voc. stands outside the sentence, and cannot be followed
directly by δέ.

4. πατήρ, of Zeus, is also used by Hephaestus (17), and Hermes
(979).

5. λεωργόν, *wilful,* is derived by Curtius through λᾱ-ϝοργός (cf.
νᾱϝος—νεώς) from the roots seen in λάω and ἔργον, ὄργανον.

6. For the absence of caesura cf. 113, 667. There are some 16 such lines in Aeschylus, 7 of them in the Persae.

10. For ὡς ἄν, ὅπως ἄν with the subj. in final clauses v. G. 1367. (Such clauses are originally conditional relative clauses, lit. 'in the way in which he may so be taught.')

11. φιλανθρώπου τρόπου, *championship of man* (Glazebrook). The sarcastic phrase is repeated in a matter-of-fact way by Hephaestus, 28.

12. σφῷν, *for you*, as far as regards you two: G. 1172.

13. ἔχει τέλος δή, *is indeed fulfilled:* so τέλος λαμβάνειν = τελεῖσθαι. Δή often marks a reference to the statement of another person, either assenting (as here to ll. 1—3, and in 42), or implying doubt, *as alleged, ostensibly*, or in questions, as 271, 314 καὶ σὺ δή, *hast thou then too?*

[For δή assenting to a command, v. 54, 57. Other uses are (1) to mark a result reached, *finally*, 243, 473, 683, 840, 874, 954, (2) as a connecting particle, *so, then*, 232, 516, (3) to lay stress on a single word, 119, 158, 441, 987.]

ἐμποδών, sc. ἐστὶ σφῷν, *hinders, detains you.*

14. συγγενῆ: Hephaestus was according to Homer (Il. 1. 577) the son of Zeus and Hera, or according to Hesiod (Theog. 927) the offspring of Hera alone; Hera was the daughter of Cronus (ib. 454), the son of Uranus. Uranus was the father of Themis (ib. 135), the mother of Prometheus.

17. ἐξωριάζειν, *disregard*, ἔξω ὥρας καὶ φροντίδος ποιεῖσθαι schol. The word does not occur elsewhere, but there seems no reason to doubt it. It implies an adj. ἔξωρος from ὥρα beside that from ὥρα: v. LS. εὔωρος, εὐωριάζω.

18. Θέμιδος: v. p. xvi.

19. ἄκοντά σ' ἄκων, *albeit loath as thyself:* so 234, 698. For other examples of this juxtaposition of two cases of the same word, so common in Greek poetry, v. 29, 208, 292, 788, 953.

21. φωνήν (sc. ἀκούσει), κ.τ.λ. a zeugma. For the postponement of του βροτῶν, which goes with φωνὴν as well as μορφήν, cf. 473 f., 1048.

22. σταθευτός, from στατός and εὔω, properly *grilled.*

23. ἀσμένῳ σοι: for this idiomatic use of a part. denoting willingness or the like in agreement with a dat. of interest depending on εἶναι or a vb. meaning *to come* or *occur*, v. G. 1584.

26. ἀεὶ δὲ κ.τ.λ., briefly for ἀεὶ δὲ παρέσται κακόν τι οὗ ἀχθηδὼν τρύσει σε, *And evermore each hour shall have its pang whose smart shall torture thee.*

27. ὁ λωφήσων κ.τ.λ.. The speaker means merely 'There is no one that can bring relief' (for the idiomatic fut. part. cf. 797 ὁ λύσων), but this is so expressed as to be almost an unconscious prophecy, for the words admit that a deliverer may be born hereafter: as to which v. 797 ff.

29 f. θεῶν goes with τιμὰς as well as with χόλον: v. 82 f.

32. κάμπτων γόνυ, regularly of resting, cf. 412, Il. 7. 118 φημί νιν ἀσπασίως γόνυ κάμψειν, εἴ κε φύγῃσιν | δηίου ἐκ πολέμοιο.

39. ὁμιλία: for the association of Hephaestus with Prometheus, see pp. ix, f.

41. πῶς οὐ, cf. 614, 785. Some edd. write οἷόν τε πῶς; οὐ τοῦτο...: cf. 275.

42. ἀεί γε δή, *Ay, thou art ever.*

43. θρηνεῖσθαι probably mid., as Soph. Aj. 852 ἀλλ᾽ οὐδὲν ἔργον ταῦτα θρηνεῖσθαι μάτην: so κλαίεσθαι, στένεσθαι in Aesch. τόνδε will then of course be the object.

44. τὰ μηδὲν ὠφελοῦντα...πόνει, *exert unavailing efforts*; the phrase lies half way, between the proper cognate acc., πονεῖν πόνον, and the adverbial acc. n. pl. of an adj. like ἀνήνυτα πονεῖν. (For μηδέν with a part. equivalent to a conditional relative clause v. G. 1612.)

45. χειρωναξία: χειρῶναξ (Hdt., Soph.) *master of his hands,* for *handicraftsman,* looks like a piece of popular humour stereotyped; cf. κώπης ἄναξ, *oarsman,* and similar periphrases with ἄναξ and ἀνάσσειν in the tragedians.

47. τέχνη = χειρωναξία, *thy craft.*

48. λαχεῖν: for the allotment of functions among the gods v. 244 ff.

49. ἅπαντ᾽ ἐπαχθῆ: *all stations have their burdens, save ruling over the gods.* Ἐπαχθής, which does not occur elsewhere in tragedy, has its literal sense, from which its usual meaning of *annoying, offensive* is derived.—κοιρανεῖν, like 972 ἄρχειν and other vbs. of *governing,* which take the gen. in prose, in the poets, especially Homer, are sometimes constructed with the dat. [It may be classed with the dat. of interest, *to be ruler for,* G. 1164; or possibly as locative, *to rule among,* Monro, H. G. § 145.]

51. ἔγνωκα τοῖσδε, *I know it from these fetters* (or possibly *this present case,* with a gesture indicating Prometheus). For the causal dat. cf. Il. 5. 182 ἀσπίδι γιγνώσκων, *recognizing him by his shield.*

54. καὶ δή, *well,* introduces a reply complying with a command: cf. 75, and δή alone in 57.

[For δή marking assent v. 13 n. The καί is *also*: the fulfilment takes place *as well as* the command; cf. οὕτω καί, and phrases like Thuc. 2. 93 ὡς δὲ ἔδοξε, καὶ ἐχώρουν, where καί is equivalent to *accordingly*.

Καὶ δή introducing a supposition is really the same: e.g. Eur. Med. 1065 καὶ δὴ τέθνασι, *but suppose I slay them*, lit. *well then, they are dead*, complying with the speaker's own suggestion that she shall murder her children.]

ψάλια, properly *curb-rings*, cf. 582 χαλινοῖς ἐν πετρίνοισι. The v. l. ψέλια, *bracelets*, is in origin the same word.

55 f. *Cast them around his arms and with might and main smite with thy hammer, rivet them to the rocks.* νιν = αὐτά. The tragg. use it in all genders and both s. and pl. θεῖνε, πασσάλευε : for the asyndeton where a second vb. reinforces the sense of the first, in a tone of impatience or insistence, cf. 58, 146, 408, 634, 724, 969. θεῖνε is applied to the chains, as in 76, though it properly applies to the bolts, πάσσαλοι, with which the chains were made fast to the rock.

57. δή = καὶ δή (v. 55 n.), so 1030, and cf. also 657.

61. καί, *also*.

62. σοφιστής, *a sage*, v. LS.; in Aesch. the word still has its general sense of a master of wisdom or of some art, with the implied idea of the public display of ability; this implication facilitates the sarcastic use of the word here and in 976, and led to its later meaning of professional teacher.

63. I.e. 'There, I have done my task so well that, except the victim of it, no one (not even Zeus, v. 77) can fairly find fault.'

64 f. Prometheus is chained against a rock and pinned to it by a wedge driven through his chest. In Hesiod Theog. 521, he is chained to a pillar, δῆσε δ' ἀλυκτοπέδῃσι Προμηθέα ποικιλόβουλον | δεσμοῖς ἀργαλέοισι μέσον διὰ κίον' ἐλάσσας ('passing the chains through the middle of a pillar '); and he so appears on an archaic vase. Wecklein thinks that this idea was derived from an early form of the story that spoke of the mountain on which Prometheus was chained figuratively as a pillar (cf. 364 n.). He notes that another vase represents him as impaled on a pillar, and supposes this to be due to a misconstruction of Hesiod. Aesch. seems to combine chaining and impalement, modifying the latter to transfixion with a wedge.

68. ὅπως μή and ὅπως with the fut. indic. in the 2nd person (and sometimes the 1st and 3rd) are used in Attic without a preceding σκόπει or ὅρα, to express a warning or command : v. G. 1352. The idiom is colloquial, and rare in poetry.

69 possibly should be written as a question.

73. **ἤ μήν**, *verily*, *I swear*, in strong asseveration, cf. 180, 939. **καί...γε πρός**, *aye, and...as well*, cf. 323, 649.

ἐπιθωΰξω : this word or **θωΰσσω** recurs 293, 409, 1073, but only once besides in Aesch., Ag. 884 (893) of a gnat buzzing; it seems to denote a shrill cry, and according to the schol. was specially used of huntsmen cheering on their hounds : cf. Eur. Hipp. 219 κυσὶ θωΰξαι.

74. **χώρει κάτω** implies that Hephaestus had climbed up the rock to fasten the giant's arms.

75. **καὶ δή**, v. 54 n.

76. **θείνε...πέδας**, cf. 56 n. **διατόρους** is probably pass., *pierced* (i.e. with holes to receive the bolts that were driven into the rock); so Soph. O. T. 1034 δ. ποδοῖν ἀκμάς of the nail-pierced ankles of Oedipus. Elsewhere it is act., but means *piercing, thrilling*—e.g. 195 δ. φόβος, Eum. 570 (567) δ. σάλπιγξ—, not *wearing, galling*, the sense appropriate here; **διατείρω** does not occur, but would apparently mean *wear through* in the sense of *pierce*, not of *wear out*.

81. **κώλοισιν**, a poetic loc. dat., made clear by **ἀμφίβληστρ' ἔχει** : cf. the dat. with ἀμφιβάλλειν 55, 71. **ἀμφίβληστρα**, *toils*, v. LS.

86. **σε δεῖ προμηθέως**: this acc. of the person (in place of the usual dat. of interest), with δεῖ and the gen. of the thing wanted, is confined to poetry; it may be on the analogy of δεῖ with the acc. and inf. (G. 1115). **προμηθέως** : the significance of the name is brought out by making it into a common noun, cf. Ag. 1064 (1085) Ἄπολλον...ἀπόλλων ἐμός· ἀπώλεσας γάρ....

87. **ὅτῳ τρόπῳ** depends directly on **προμηθέως**=τοῦ προμηθησομένου. **τέχνης**=τεχνήματος, *handiwork*, schol. τῶν δεσμῶν.

90. **γέλασμα** betokens the flashing of ripples in the sun (ridet placidi pellacia ponti, Lucr., Keble's ' many-twinkling smile of ocean '), not their plashing on the beach (καχλάζειν, cachinni undarum in Catullus). The primary idea of γελᾶν is brightness, not sound: Il. 19. 362 γέλασσε δὲ πᾶσα περὶ χθὼν | χαλκοῦ ὑπὸ στεροπῆς.

93. The outburst of feeling is marked by the transition to anapaests, chanted in recitative. The impression is heightened by the pause or 'rest' for the length of 2 feet after the half-line 97, as at 126 and 128. L. 101 reverts to spoken iambics, as calmer thoughts prevail.

99. **πῆμα στενάχω, πῇ**.... For the loosely dependent interrogative cf. 197. In the normal form, e.g. 320 ff., 669 ff., (1) the subj. of the dependent verb is the same as the object of the main verb; (2) the dependent clause is in apposition with the accusative, and could stand

alone as the object of the main verb; cf. 1127 ἐσορᾷς μ' ὡς ἔκδικα πάσχω with 146 ἐσίδεσθ' οἵῳ δεσμῷ...φρουρὰν ὀχήσω.

100. **τέρματα** = τέρμα, a common but specially curious case of the 'pluralis majestaticus'; cf. 737 σκῆπτρα, 793 θρόνων. **ἐπιτείλαι**, *come round, arise,* especially of the stars; usually in the pass., but the act. intr. is quoted from the Little Iliad λαμπρὴ δ' ἐπέτελλε σελήνη: cf. ἀνατέλλω intr. (When trans. it means *enjoin* or *ordain,* but hardly *fix,* as LS. suggest,—in the sense that would be required here of *forecast.*)—*Oh, where* (or *how*) *shall the dawn of my release appear?*

101 f. **πάντα προυξεπίσταμαι** κ.τ.λ. : in 281 ff. Prometheus repeats this statement with some qualification; and from 225 and 899 it appears that he only knew the future so far as it was imparted to him by his mother Themis.

106. **οὔτε σιγᾶν** is explained by what follows, **θνητοῖς γὰρ** κ.τ.λ. ; **οὔτε μὴ σιγᾶν** by what precedes: indignation prompts utterance, resignation silence. A similar thought is expressed in 213 f.

108. **ἀνάγκαις**: both s. and pl. regularly of personal violence and torture, v. LS. *This yoke of torment has been bound upon me.*

109 f. **δέ** introduces as simply a fresh statement what is really an explanation of **θνητοῖς γέρα πορών**: cf. Pers. 145 (142) φροντίδα κεδνὴν θώμεθα· χρεία δὲ προσήκει. *A fennel-stalk filled full I make my prey, a furtive source of fire,—revealed to men as teacher of all crafts, a mighty means.* **ναρθηκοπλήρωτον**: cf. πληροῦν οἶνον ἐς ἄγγος, and pass. πληροῦσθαι ἐς, of people *crowding into* a place (Eur.). **θηρῶμαι**, 'graphic' pres. for aor., cf. 245. **πηγὴν πυρός** cf. 834 ἡλίου πηγαῖς of the east. **κλοπαίαν** is poetic for κεκλεμμένην.—For the legend v. pp. x. f.

113. For the absence of caesura, if the text be right, v. 6 n.

116. **προσέπτα**, here trans., as are often verbs of motion compounded with a prep., e.g. 132 προσέβα. In 574 and 671 προσπέτομαι takes the dative.—**ἀφεγγής**, *rayless,* in the sense of *unseen,* is transferred to ἀχώ and ὀδμά from their origin. So also is **κεκραμένη**: *from god, or man, or mixed of both,* i.e. or coming from a being half-way between god and man (like the Oceanides): cf. Eur. Hel. 1137 θεὸς ἢ μὴ θεὸς ἢ τὸ μέσον.

118 f. **ἵκετο**: the subj. is implied in the last line; **θεωρός** is predicative, being parallel to τί δὴ θέλων ;

120. **ὁρᾶτε**: the plural keeps up the vagueness.

122. **δι' ἀπεχθείας ἐλθόντα** = ἀπεχθῆ γενόμενον: cf. δι' ἔχθρας μολεῖν, διὰ μάχης ἐλθεῖν &c. c. dat.

123. **εἰσοιχνεῦσιν**: the Ionic contraction is appropriate to the Epic verb, cf. 672 πωλεύμεναι, Eur. Hipp. 167 ἀύτευν.

128. **ὑποσυρίζει**, *hums with the soft pulsation of wings*; ὑπο- denotes *in accompaniment to*, as in ὑπᾴδειν, ὑπορχεῖσθαι, and 596 ὑποτοβεῖ.

134. **μόγις παρειποῦσα**: Aesch. assigns to the daughters of Oceanus the secluded life that Athenian maidens led in his own day, and not the greater freedom of the Homeric ladies. Sophocles attributes similar ideas of feminine propriety to the times of Electra and Antigone (v. Jebb on Ant. 578).

140. **σύθην**: the tragg. often omit the syllabic augment in messengers' speeches and in lyrics, less often and only in lyrics the temporal, as 194 ἐρέθισε. Both augments are often omitted by Homer and the Lyric poets.—**ἀπέδιλος**, owing to their haste; cf. Theocr. 19. 36 (Alcmena to Amphitryon) ἄνστα, μηδὲ πόδεσσιν ἑοῖς ὑπὸ σάνδαλα θείης. The Greeks went barefoot indoors.

144. **ἀκοιμήτῳ**, i.e. ever flowing. In Il. 14. 243 ff. Hypnos boasts that any other of the gods but Zeus he could easily lull to sleep, *even the streams of the river Oceanus, the parent of them all.*

146 ff. **δεσμῷ προσπορπατὸς…σκοπέλοισιν**, cf. the datives with προσπασσαλεύειν 20.

151 f. **φοβερά**, the passive sense *frightened* transferred to something *caused by fear*, cf. Thuc. 4. 128. 4 φοβερὰ ἀναχώρησις. **προσῇξε**, 'instantaneous' aor., v. 194 n. *And from alarm there has rushed to my eyes a mist of welling tears, to see....*

153. **εἰσιδοῦσαν**, as though οἶκτος ὑπῆλθέ με preceded. This syntax is not uncommon: cf. Pers. 915 (913) λέλυται γὰρ ἐμῶν γυίων ῥώμη... ἐσιδόντα.

155. **ταῖσδ' ἀδαμαντοδέτοισι λύμαις**, *these shameful bonds of steel*, cf. 603 οἰστρηλάτῳ δείματι.

156. **νέοι οἰακονόμοι**: the plural is vague, Zeus only being meant.

159. **ἀθέτως κρατύνει**, *holdeth uncovenanted sway*, the opposite of a constitutional ruler, cf. 202, 340, 419.

161. **εἰ γάρ** and εἴθε are used with the imperfect or aorist indicative of an unfulfilled wish referring to present or past time, G. 1511.

166 f. **ὡς ἐπεγήθει**: the imperfect or aorist indicative in final clauses denotes that the purpose is not or was not attained, as it depends on an act that does not or did not take place; cf. 775 f., and G. 1371. *Would he had sent me under ground...that neither god nor any other should be exulting at my state.* **ἐπεγήθει**: the present-stem, used by Homer, occurs also Cho. 768 (772) γαθούσῃ φρενί: perhaps here also we should

write it with the old Attic ᾱ. Elsewhere in Attic the perfect γέγηθα is used for the present.

167. **αἰθέριον κίνυγμα**, *the sport of the breezes:* κίνυγμα (κινύσσομαι frequentative of κινεῖσθαι, cf. αἴνιγμα, αἰνίσσομαι, αἰνέω) is explained by scholia here and elsewhere as εἴδωλον, and may have signified something like the Lat. *oscillum*, a little mask or figure hung on trees at rural festivals as a charm to bring fertility (Virg. Georg. 2. 382 ff., Prop. 4. 1. 18).

171. **ξυνασχαλᾷ**: the Homeric ἀσχαλάω occurs also at 259, 790 (where however v. crit. n.), and Eur. I. A. 920. Elsewhere, as 319, ἀσχάλλω is used in Attic, as once in Homer.

174. **θέμενος ἄγναμπτον νόον**, so Il. 9. 629 ἄγριον ἐν στήθεσσι θέτο μεγαλήτορα θυμόν, Tyrt. 11. 5 ἐχθρὰν μὲν ψυχὴν θέμενος, and cf. 543; θεῖναι, *to make*, becomes θέσθαι when the object concerns oneself.

175. **Οὐρανίαν**, *of Uranus*, cf. 681 Δῖον, *of Zeus.*

183. *To reveal the new project* (i.e. on the part of Zeus himself, cf. 788) *as a result whereof:* this is the first hint of Prometheus' secret, that leads to the catastrophe of the play.

184. **ἀποσυλᾶται**, 'prophetic' pres. (the future being present to the prophet), cf. 227, 529, 799, 793, 874. So in Eng. we might say, 'If Zeus executes his project, he *loses* his throne.'

185. The absence of the diaeresis or division between the two halves of the line is to be noticed.

194. **ἐρέθισε**: the 'instantaneous' aorist is used of a sudden access of feeling: the feeling is still present, but its commencement is already past. Similarly ἐπήνεσα, *good!* ἀπέπτυσα (1103), *I loathe*, &c. For the absence of the augment v. 140 n.

201. **ἀπαράμυθον**, metri gratia, after the Epic manner; so ἀκάματον Pers. 903 (901), and ἀθάνατος regularly in Attic poetry as in Homer. [The lengthening was facilitated by the earlier form of the prefix, ἀν-, which survived before a vowel.]

202 f. **παρ' ἑαυτῷ τὸ δίκαιον ἔχων**, *keeping the rules of law to himself*, i.e. secret: the absence of published laws and principles of justice being the characteristic of arbitrary rule. So Eur. Supp. 430 (under a tyranny) οὐκ εἰσιν νόμοι | κοινοί, κρατεῖ δ' εἷς τὸν νόμον κεκτημένος | αὐτὸς παρ' αὐτῷ. Cf. 159 n.

203. **ὄίω**: the act. is epic.

205. **ταύτῃ**, *in that wise*, i.e. as I said.

209. **γέγωνε**: this imperative (which occurs also 810), with the subjunctive γεγώνω (Soph.) and infinitive γεγωνέμεν (Il.), freq. γεγω-

νίσκειν (654), suggests a present (γεγώνω) side by side with the perfect γέγωνα: cf. ἄνωγα, ἄνωγε, ἀνωγέμεν. There is also the form (γεγωνέω) γεγωνεῖν (539, 684, 813, 846) and γεγωνῆσαι (1022). The word is found in no other play of Aeschylus.

217. οἱ μὲν κ.τ.λ., as though ἐστασίαζον ἐν ἀλλήλοις preceded.

218. δῆθεν, as 1018, indignant, *that Zeus might reign forsooth.* The emphasis is perhaps partly on ἀνάσσοι, Zeus's tyranny contrasted with the paternal rule of Cronus.

[Δῆθεν is possibly δή + θεν, a short form of the Homeric θήν, *assuredly*, cf. μέν, μήν. It may simply emphasize a phrase, without implying feeling. It is also used like inverted commas, to mark a profession as distinct from a fact,—either simply or implying doubt. See F. W. Thomas in *Cl. Rev.* VIII. 441.]

219. ἄρξειεν, *come to rule*, cf. 224 δεσπόσειν, *should gain the mastery.* The aor. and fut. of vbs. denoting a *state* may express *entrance into* that state : G. 1260.

220 ff. Two interpretations seem possible : (1) *advising for the best could not persuade the Titans*, for τὰ λῷστα βουλεύων Τιτᾶσιν, οὐκ ἠδυνήθην πιθεῖν αὐτούς, the order being due to a desire to bring together the contrasted βουλεύων and πιθεῖν ; (2) *purposing to persuade the Titans for the best, did not succeed* (so βουλεύω c. inf. Soph. El. 649, Eur. And. 806); but then βουλεύων πιθεῖν merely = πείθων, so that the balance is in favour of (1).

221. Χθονός = Γαίας, so Eum. 6.

224. πρὸς βίαν, *with reference to*, i.e. *by force*, = 228 πρὸς τὸ καρτερόν, cf. 510 πρὸς ἡδονήν. δεσπόσειν, v. 219 n.

225 f. Θέμις καὶ Γαῖα : in Eum. init. Aesch. makes Themis the daughter of Earth (so Hes. Th. 135), and her successor in the oracular seat at Delphi (so Paus. 10. 5. 6). The present passage is probably to be taken as identifying them, in accordance with a local Attic variation of the myth, attested by two inscriptions (C. I. A. 3. 318, 350) on seats in the theatre at Athens, appropriating them to a priestess and two ἐρσηφόροι of Ge Themis. This interpretation is supported by πολλῶν ὀνομάτων μορφὴ μία, which, if Themis and Earth are not the same person, becomes a superfluous reference to other identifications of Earth, with Demeter, Hestia, &c. See also 1125.—For καί in the sense of *seu, or*, coupling alternative names, see W. M. Ramsay in *Cl. Rev.* XII. 337.

[Against the identification, it must be noted that at 900 Θέμις is called Τιτανίς, a name applied in Eum. 6 to Phoebe as παῖς Χθονός, and so sister of the Titans, but nowhere apparently used of Earth as their mother. Also in 220 ff. Prometheus does not imply that he is a brother of the Titans : he is himself called a Titan by Soph. and Eur., but that is as son of the Titan Iapetus, a relationship that Aeschylus ignores. These considerations might point to the rejection of the line as an interpolation, for at 899 Prometheus derives his foreknowledge from Themis only.]

226. **πολλῶν ὀνομάτων μορφὴ μία**, poetic gen. of quality, equivalent to an epithet, πολυώνυμος, cf. 930 ἀλατείαις πόνων, Soph. O. T. 532 ἦ τοσόνδ' ἔχεις τόλμης πρόσωπον, *hast thou so bold a front?*

227. **κραίνοιτο**, 'prophetic' pres., cf. 184 n.; opt. in oratio obliqua as 229 χρείη, G. 1280.

228 f. **κατ' ἰσχύν**, lit. *by way of strength* (cf. κατὰ τάχος, καθ' ἡδονήν),=**πρὸς τὸ καρτερόν**, for which v. 224 n. The two adverbial phrases qualify **κρατεῖν**, which has no subject expressed until for the simple adv. δόλῳ is substituted **δόλῳ τοὺς ὑπερσχόντας** : lit. *that it was not ordained (to conquer) by strength nor violence, but that those who surpassed in guile should conquer.* For the transposition of **δόλῳ** to emphasize the antithesis, cf. Soph. O. T. 139 ὅστις γὰρ ἦν ἐκεῖνον ὁ κτανών, τάχ' ἂν | κἄμ' ἂν τοιαύτῃ χειρὶ τιμωρεῖν θέλοι, 'the slayer of Laïus might also want to take vengeance on *me.'* **ὑπερσχόντας** is the 'timeless' aor. part., giving the idea of the agent simply, as the aor. inf. may give that of the action : cf. Thuc. 1. 69. 1 ὁ δουλωσάμενος, *the enslaver.* (It can hardly be past with reference to **κρατεῖν**, *those that had surpassed should prevail.*)

[This interpretation, making the sentence develop as it goes along, seems preferable to taking **οὐ κατ'...δόλῳ δέ** as a single adverbial phrase qualifying either (1) **τοὺς ὑπερσχόντας**, *those that surpassed not by...but in guile should prevail,*—or (2) **κρατεῖν**, when **ὑπερσχόντας** would be 'inceptive' (v. 219 n.), *those that got the upper hand should prevail not by...but by guile:* but ὑπερέχειν naturally connects with a dat. in its neighbourhood.]

231. **προσβλέψαι**, *regard, consider*, sc. αὐτά, i.e. ἃ ἐξηγησάμην. **τὸ πᾶν** adv.

232. **κράτιστα τῶν παρεστώτων**, *best as things were*, lit. *of present (possibilities)*, so Ag. 1037 (1053) τὰ λῷστα τῶν παρεστώτων.—**δή**, *so, finally*, connecting, as 516.

233 ff. **προσλαβόντι** agrees with **μοι**, **ἑκόντα** with (**ἐμέ**) subj. of **συμπαρασταστεῖν**: both concords are common (e.g. Eur. Med. 1236 δέδοκταί μοι...παῖδας κτανούσῃ τῆσδ' ἀφορμᾶσθαι χθονός, | καὶ μὴ σχολὴν

ἄγουσαν ἐκδοῦναι τέκνα κ.τ.λ.), but no other case is quoted of an attributive dat. and acc. in the same clause. (In Thuc. 2. 39. 4 περιγίγνεται ἡμῖν...ἐς αὐτὰ ἐλθοῦσι μὴ ἀτολμοτέρους (v. l. -οις) φαίνεσθαι, the acc., if correct, is predicative.) The change from the dat. to the acc. here is made in order to avoid confusion with the following dat. ἑκόντι Ζηνί: v. Jebb on Ant. 546.—For ἑκόνθ' ἑκόντι v. 19 n.

236. καλύπτει, prob. 'graphic' pres., like 245 νέμει, not *still hides.*

237. αὐτοῖσι συμμάχοισι, *and his allies withal,* lit. 'with his very allies,' dat. of accompaniment, cf. 1079, G. 1189 ff. [In this phrase note (1) σύν is dispensed with, as the idiomatic αὐτοῖς indicates in which of its various senses the dat. is used, (2) the art. is usually omitted, even in prose, the idiom being stereotyped in its Homeric form.]

239. ἐξημείψατο here only in the sense of *requite fully:* cf. 1071 ἐξαμαρτάνειν *to err utterly.*

242. δ' οὖν resumes the narrative after the digression of the preceding general reflection.

245 f. Note the double change of tenses.

250. καὶ τοῖσιν: the art. in Attic occasionally retains its original pronominal use after καί and prepositions, as often with μέν, δέ and γάρ.

251 f. ἐξελυσάμην τὸ μὴ μολεῖν: vbs. denoting hindrance and similar negative ideas take either the infin. alone (as 264, 654, 1089) ; or τοῦ with the inf. expressing purpose; or τό with the inf., a sort of acc. of respect (as here, 812, 891, 950): G. 1548—51. The negation contained in the verb is repeated by the redundant μή with the inf.: G. 1615.

253. τῷ, *by this, therefore,* Homeric, cf. 250 n.

255. ἐν οἴκτῳ προθέμενος occurs here only : προ- seems to mean *beforehand, first,* as in προλαμβάνειν ; ἐν οἴκτῳ θέσθαι *to pity,* cf. Hdt. 3. 3, ἐν τιμῇ θέσθαι *to honour.* (Alone προθέσθαι means *to set in front of oneself,* or *to prefer* τί τινος.)

259. συνασχαλᾷ, v. 171 n.

261. ἠλγύνθην, for the aor. v. 194 n.

262. καὶ μήν, lit. *and verily,* seems to mean *indeed,* in assent. But this use of the particles is doubtful, and perhaps the text is corrupt: v. crit. n. (For other uses v. 475, 1014, 1114.)

263. μή = μῶν, as 991.

264. προδέρκεσθαι, found here only, seems to mean *see beforehand* in the sense of *be ever looking forward to* (δέρκεσθαι being *to fix the gaze on*). rather than *foresee;* since τυφλαὶ ἐλπίδες (266)—the sanguine

temper of men engrossed in the arts that Prometheus taught—would cure men of brooding over their fate, but not prevent their foreseeing it: so far from depriving them of foresight, Prometheus claims to have first taught men to see to any purpose (463) and to have reduced divination to a science (500). [The myth in Plato Gorg. 523 D, however, states that men had foreknowledge of, προειδέναι, the actual day of their death, until Prometheus at the command of Zeus deprived them of it.]—For μή and the inf. v. 251 n.

265. τὸ ποῖον: the art. is used with ποῖος when the thing about which the question is asked has been previously mentioned or implied, as here ἔπαυσα implies φάρμακον: cf. Soph. El. 670 πρᾶγμα πορσύνων μέγα.—Τὸ ποῖον;

266. Hesiod has a different and obscure allegory about Hope (Op. 49 ff.): in revenge for the theft of fire by Prometheus, Zeus sent a woman called Pandora to plague mankind; erstwhile men had lived free from all evils, but the woman took the lid off the jar and let them out; Hope alone was left in the jar, as she clapped the lid on before it could fly away; but countless other ills are abroad among men.

272. χαλᾷ κακῶν: in 189 we have ἐκ δισμῶν χαλάσῃ trans., *set loose* (cf. 1023 χαλασθῇ δεσμά, 58 χάλα trans. with obj. understood, *let go*); in 1090 τί χαλᾷ μανιῶν; is intr., *what does he abate of madness?* Here it is probably trans., *and gives me never a respite from pain,*— both for symmetry and because χαλᾶν κακῶν intr. would mean *abate in suffering*, not *in causing*, *ill*.

276. ἤμαρτες, *thou hast erred:* Prometheus accepts the word (282), which apparently here, as clearly ἐξαμαρτάνειν 1071, has the sense of an error of judgment rather than of a sin. The two senses are by no means kept distinct in Greek thought: hence the Socratic paradox, οὐδεὶς ἑκὼν ἁμαρτάνει.

277. καθ' ἡδονήν, more often an adv., v. 228 n., here forms an adj. predicate to (ἐστί); so ἐν ἡδονῇ and (510) πρὸς ἡδονὴν εἶναί τινι.

279 f. πημάτων ἔξω πόδα ἔχει, proverbial, cf. Cho. 693 (696) ἔξω κομίζων ὀλεθρίου πηλοῦ πόδα.

281 ff. ταῦθ' ἅπαντα, probably not *all you say*, but *all that has befallen me*, leading up to what follows. Prometheus begins a denial of the charge of error, because he foresaw the consequences of his act, and chose to suffer in the service of man; but breaks off with the admission ἥμαρτον (v. 276 n.), explained by οὐ μήν τι ποιναῖς κ.τ.λ.— he did make a mistake in so far as he did not expect the penalty to be

so severe. '(It is easy to admonish me now, and say I erred,) *but I knew all that would befall me: of my own free will—'twas an error, I shall not deny it—to aid mankind I brought trouble on myself: but still I never thought....*'

[This interpretation is suggested by that of Wecklein, who prints ἐκὼν ἐκών—ἥμαρτον, οὐκ ἀρνήσομαι· taking ἐκών with ἥμαρτον, which is substituted by a change of thought for ξυνέτυχον τούτῳ τῷ πάθει. Others give ἥμαρτον its other sense, translating *Of my own free will I sinned—if you like to call it so.* Neither version seems to explain the connexion of thought in the whole passage.]

285. **πεδαρσίοις** shows the Doric (also Lesbian and Boeotian) πεδά for μετά: Aesch. also uses πεδάορος, πέδοικος and πεδαίχμιος.

287. **καί μοι...μή,** Ethic dat.; so often μή μοι.

288. **πέδοι δὲ βᾶσαι,** *alighting on the ground,* cf. 775 πέδοι σκήψασα, 'Αλφεῷ μέσσῳ καταβάς Pind. Ol. 6. 58, and the loc. and locatival dat. with πίπτω in poetry, χαμαί, πεδίῳ πέσε Il.—**τὰς προσερπούσας τύχας** Prometheus does not actually recount till 783 ff., 897 ff., but the invitation here gives the necessary opportunity for the Chorus to take its place in the orchestra.

289. **διὰ τέλους** is idiomatically used for διὰ παντὸς μέχρι τέλους.

291 f. **νῦν** is explained by what follows: later it may be your turn to suffer. **ταῦτά,** *in the same way,* cogn. acc. as though with ἄλλοτε ἄλλος πημαίνεται. **πρὸς ἄλλοτ' ἄλλον:** cf. 19 n., and for the order cf. 788 πρὸς αὐτὸς αὐτοῦ.

293. **ἐπεθώυξας:** v. 73 n.

295 f. **κραιπνόσυντον θᾶκον,** the ὄχος πτερωτός (140).

300. **δολιχῆς:** for the inconsistency with 132—8, and also the curious fact that Oceanus ignores his daughters' presence, v. pp. xxiii. f.

τέρμα κελεύθου (instead of κέλευθον) **διαμειψάμενος,** cf. 849 τὸ πᾶν πορείας τέρμα for τὴν πᾶσαν πορείαν, and 289 διὰ τέλους.

305. **τὸ ξυγγενές:** Oceanus was the son of Uranus and Ge (Hes. Theog. 133).

307 f. **οὐκ ἔστιν ὅτῳ νείμαιμι:** the potential opt. without ἄν after ἔστιν ὅστις, ὅπως, ὅποι, is poetic; cf. Ag. 625 (620) οὐκ ἔσθ' ὅπως λέξαιμι τὰ ψευδῆ καλά. G. 1333.—**μοῖραν νέμειν,** *to pay respect;* so Soph. Trach. 1238 οὐ νέμει πατρὶ | φθίνοντι μοῖραν (with no qualifying adj.): '*μοῖρα* is the share of respect due to a person' (Jebb).

312. **Ὠκεανοῦ:** the reference to himself in the 3rd person, while serving to let the audience know who he is, has a sound at once hearty and pompous that is in keeping with his character. He is fond of

proverbial phrases (325, 334 f., 337 'you make bad worse,' 339, 345, 352, 394, 401) and homely turns of expression (335 τἀπίχειρα, 339 κῶλον ἐκτείνειν for λακτίζειν, 341 εἶμι καὶ πειράσομαι, 345 προστρίβεται)..

315. **πῶς ἐτόλμησας**, *how hast thou ventured*, refers to the length of the journey, l. 300; also no doubt Oceanus seldom left his abode, since he or his stream (they are distinguished here, but not so clearly above, 145—7) was the bond that held the world together: in Il. 20. 7 he is the only river absent from the council of the gods.

317. **αὐτόκτιτ'** = *self built, natural*, or perhaps *made by thyself*, i.e. hollowed by the waves.— **σιδηρομήτορα** of Scythia, v. 740 n.

318. **ἦ** introduces a reply suggested by the speaker himself to his own question: *can you have come to gaze?*

320. **τόνδε**, of the speaker, as often in tragedy ὅδ' ἀνήρ.

322. **ὑπ' αὐτοῦ** emphatic, *by himself*, the very god I aided; cf. 374, 376 n.

323. **καὶ...γε**, *and moreover*, cf. 73 n.

325. **γίγνωσκε σαυτόν**, *learn what thou art*, an adaptation of the maxim γνῶθι σεαυτόν, *know thyself*, inscribed at the entrance to the temple of Apollo at Delphi, and sometimes ascribed to the Seven Sages (Mayor on Juv. 11. 27, Frazer on Paus. 10. 24. 1).

μεθάρμοσαι, *reform*; **νεούς** is proleptic.

327 ff. **εἰ...ῥίψεις, τάχ' ἄν...κλύοι**: note protasis and apodosis in different forms. G. 1421.

329 f. **τὸν νῦν *ὄχλον παρόντα**: this inverted order is common in Thuc., e.g. 1. 90. 1 τὴν εἰς τὸν Μηδικὸν πόλεμον τόλμαν γενομένην. For ὄχλον μόχθων cf. 853 ὄχλον λόγων.

333. **ἀρχαῖα...λέγειν τάδε**, *perchance 'twill seem to thee an outworn saw*, i.e. the reference that follows to the proverbial punishment of pride. Ἀρχαιολογεῖν is similarly used, Thuc. 7. 69. 2.

339. **πρὸς κέντρα κ.τ.λ.**, v. LS. s. v. λακτίζειν.

341 f. **πειράσομαι ἐάν**: the common use of a condition expressing purpose; cf. Il. 5. 279 ἐγχείῃ πειρήσομαι, αἴ κε τύχωμι, *try with my spear, if haply I may hit*, Plat. Legg. 638 E πειρώμενος ἂν ἄρα δύνωμαι δηλοῦν. G. 1420. [It is not an indirect question, but a protasis that implies an apodosis stating the purpose: *try (that I may release), if I can release*. M. and T. 486 ff.]

346. **ζηλῶ σε**, *I envy thee*, in a tone of some contempt for one who has safely sided with the powers that be; taken with the next l. it is equivalent to 'take care lest you implicate yourself by sympathizing with me.'

347. **πάντων μετασχὼν κ.τ.λ.**, *albeit thou sharedst all and hast* *dared all with me*, a sarcastic exaggeration of the fellowship implied in Oceanus's professions of sympathy, 304 ff.; cf. 315 πῶς ἐτόλμησας... Actually, Prometheus claims to have stood alone in his resistance to Zeus, 250. **μετασχὼν καὶ τετολμηκώς** have the same construction, **πάντων ἐμοί**, as μετασχών alone would have, μετα- applying to both participles; συν- is similarly carried on in Soph. Ant. 537 καὶ ξυμμετίσχω καὶ φέρω τῆς αἰτίας and Eur. I. T. 684 χρὴ συνεκπνεῦσαί μέ σοι καὶ συσφαγῆναι καὶ πυρωθῆναι δέμας.

348. **μηδέ σοι μελησάτω**: the 3rd person of the aor. imp. in prohibitions (for the usual pres. imp. or aor. subj.) is not so rare as the 2nd (G. 1347).

350. **ὁδῷ**, *by the errand*, for the dat. cf. 212 βλάπτῃ λόγῳ.

356. **τὰ μέν** is taken up by **ἀτάρ. σ' ἐπαινῶ**, almost equivalent to *I thank you;* like *merci* and *ich danke*, it was used as a polite refusal, Ar. Ran. 508 κάλλιστ', ἐπαινῶ. **λήξω**, sc. ἐπαινῶν.

361. **εἵνεκα**, the epic form of ἕνεκα, used metri gratia in trag., cf. 143 εἰλισσομένου, and ξεῖνος, μοῦνος &c.

[**Οὕνεκα**, i.e. οὗ ἕνεκα, properly a conj., appears as a prep. in Attic verse inscrr. as well as εἵνεκα: both are attested by MSS. in Aesch. and Eur., οὕνεκα alone in Soph. Kühner-Blass, *Gr. Gr.* I. 2, p. 251.]

363. **οὐ δῆτ' ἐπεί** in the middle of a speech as in Soph. O.C. 431 εἴποις ἂν ὡς...οὐ δῆτ', ἐπεί τοι...and elsewhere.

κασιγνήτου: according to Hesiod, Theog. 509 ff., Atlas and Prometheus were sons of Iapetus and Clymene. Aesch. keeps their relationship, although he makes Prometheus the son of Themis and does not mention his father.

364. **πρὸς ἑσπέρους τόπους**, *towards*, i.e. *near*.

Atlas, 'the bearer' (τλάω), revolted with the Titans against Zeus, who in punishment set him to support the sky. ('It is a very common idea among primitive peoples...that the sky used to lie flat down on the earth, till it was pushed up by some strong man, or wonderful animal or plant'—Frazer, *Pausanias*, III. p. 541.) Hesiod places him in the far west (hence the name of the Atlantic), and pictures him simply as 'holding the broad heaven on his head and untiring hands' (Theog. 517, 746). In Od. 1. 53 he 'knows the depths of all the sea, and holds (i.e., probably, guards) by himself the tall pillars that hold both earth and sky apart,' θαλάσσης | πάσης βένθεα οἶδεν, ἔχει δέ τε κίονας αὐτὸς | μακράς, αἳ γαῖάν τε καὶ οὐρανὸν ἀμφὶς ἔχουσιν. How Aeschylus conceives his burden is not clear. **κίον' οὐρανοῦ τε καὶ χθονός**, 'the sky-and-earth pillar,' is usually interpreted *the pillar between earth and sky*, supporting the sky, resting on the earth and propped by Atlas's shoulders. But the words more naturally mean *the pillar supporting both sky and earth,* either propped or entirely carried by Atlas, whose ποῦ στῶ is not determined (Homer *loc. cit.* might be taken as placing him at the bottom of the sea). One account—no doubt later than the primitive conception given in Hesiod—did make Atlas support the earth as well as the sky: ἐπὶ τῶν ὤμων κατὰ τὰ λεγόμενα οὐρανόν τε ἀνέχει καὶ γῆν writes Pausanias (2nd c. A.D.) in his Guide to Greece, 5. 18. 4, describing a painting on the Chest of Cypselus at Olympia, a work dating perhaps a century before Aeschylus[1].—In Herodotus (4. 184) Atlas appears rationalized as a cloud-capped mountain in Libya, said by the natives to be ὁ κίων τοῦ οὐρανοῦ.

367 ff. In one or two points this passage may have been inspired by Pindar's description of Typho and of the eruption of Etna, Pyth. 1. 15—28, with which it should be compared.

368. **δάιον,** *destructive,* connected with δαίω *to burn,* and specially applied in Homer to fire, so appropriate here. (The other sense, *wretched,* shows a passive use, lit. *consumed.*)

371. **συρίζων φόβον,** *hissing terror,* poetic for συρίζων φοβερὸν συριγμόν: cf. Sept. 373 (386) κλάζουσι κώδωνες φόβον, and βλέπειν ᾿Αρη &c. (G. 1055).

374,6. **αὐτῷ, αὐτόν** emphatic, '(while flashing lightnings to destroy another) there came upon *himself* a bolt...that smote *him* down.' Cf. 941, and Soph. Phil. 314 τοιαῦτ' ᾿Ατρεῖδαί με...δεδράκασ', οἵ᾿Ολύμπιοι θεοὶ | δοῖέν ποτ᾿ αὐτοῖς ἀντίποιν᾿ ἐμοῦ παθεῖν.

375. **καταιβάτης,** a regular epithet of Zeus, as descending in the thunderbolt, here transferred to **κεραυνός,** as in 374 **ἄγρυπνον** to **βέλος.**

377. **φρένας** in its literal sense, the midriff; *to his very vitals.*

378. **σθένος,** 'retained' acc. with **ἐξεβροντήθη,** on the analogy of vbs. of *depriving,* e.g. 787 σκῆπτρα συληθήσεται: the act. would be

---

[1] Pausanias gives the same description of another picture of Atlas at Olympia, on the throne of Zeus made in the time of Pericles. His interpretation of the painting on the Chest differs from the legend beneath it, which he records: ᾿Ατλας οὐρανὸν οὗτος ἔχει, τὰ δὲ μᾶλα μεθήσει. But it is rash to deny his accuracy (as is done e.g. in Roscher's *Lexikon,* p. 706, and Preller-Robert's *Mythologie,* p. 562) and suppose that both pictures really showed Atlas carrying the sky only. In extant works of art it is not till later times that his load appears as a starry globe: in the earlier vase-paintings it is vaguely indicated as a rock (Roscher, p. 710), and in the metope at Olympia, where Heracles has taken Atlas's place, his burden (τὸ φόρημα as Pausanias cautiously calls it, 5. 10. 9) was represented by the upper part of the entablature in which the sculpture was set (Gardner, *Handbook of Greek Sculpture,* p. 228).

Ζεὺς ἐξεβρόντησεν αὐτὸν τὸ σθένος, 'blasted-the-strength-out-of him' (G. 1239); but the balance of the line would show that it goes also with ἐφεψαλώθη, which alone would hardly take an acc.; v. 347 n. So Mrs Browning, 'For stricken to the very soul, his strength was scorch'd and thunder-blasted from him.'

383. This is doubtless an allusion to the eruption of Etna that occurred in 479 B.C.; v. p. xxvii.

386. ἐξαναζέσει χόλον, an extended use of the cogn. acc.

394. ὀργῆς, *temper, mind*, cp. 80 ὀργῆς τραχύτητα.

400 f. I.e. 'If this be folly, let me be foolish; better be thought a fool than be one!' For νόσῳ νοσεῖν of mental ailment cf. 1009 f.

402. τἀμπλάκημα, the offence of pleading with Zeus.

404. θρῆνος οὑμός, *lamentation for me:* the possess. adj. pron. is occasionally equivalent to the obj. gen. G. 999.

405. θακοῦντι παγκρατεῖς ἕδρας, *enthron'd in sovran state*, probably cogn. acc., ἕδρας being abstract, *posture* (as in Soph. O. T. 2 τίνας ποθ' ἕδρας τάσδε μοι θοάζετε ; *why sit ye here before me ?* and Eur. Rhes. 512 ἵζειν κλωπικὰς ἕδρας), not concrete, *seat* (though vbs. of sitting can take the acc. of the thing sat on, as Eur. Or. 956 τρίποδα καθίζειν, I. T. 277 θάσσειν φάραγγα). For the plur. cf. 100 n.

408. τὸν παρόντα νοῦν, *thy present purpose* of returning home.

409. ἐθώϋξας, v. 73 n.

410. ψαίρει, *fans*, lightly beats (not *grazes*, *scrapes*, as LS., q. v., and cf. διαψαίρω). The vb. is usually intr., and according to the schol. is specially used of sails flapping in a light breeze. The 'four-legged bird fans with his pinions the smooth highway of air,' as an ordinary horse would paw the ground.

411. τἄν=τοι ἄν.

412. κάμψειεν γόνυ, v. 32 n.

413 f. στένω...τύχας : the gen. of cause is common with verbs of emotion, e.g. Soph. El. 1027 ζηλῶ σε τοῦ νοῦ, τῆς δὲ δειλίας στυγῶ : G. 1126.

416. ῥαδινὸν ῥέος : the precise meaning is not clear. Hesychius explains ῥαδινός as λεπτός, ἰσχνός, εὐκίνητός, ἁπαλός, and the translation *slender* suits most of its uses; here perhaps it denotes a thin *trickling stream* of tears.

418 ff. ἀμέγαρτα τάδε κρατύνων, cogn. acc., cf. 44 n.—ἰδίοις νόμοις, cf. 158.—θεοῖς τοῖς πάρος, Cronus and the Titans.—αἰχμάν, in the sense of *temper, impulse*, from ἀίσσω, is possibly a different word etymologically from αἰχμή in its other senses : v. LS.—*Untoward is this reign of*

arbitrary law, and proud the spirit Zeus displays towards the gods of old.

423. στονόεν λέλακε: cf. Il. 6. 484 δακρυόεν γελάσασα.

424 ff. μεγαλοσχήμονα and ἀρχαιοπρεπῆ go closely with στένουσι, and <*men*> *lament the pride and ancient glories of thine and of thy kinsmen's high estate.* A subject to στένουσι is wanting, and comparison with the strophe shows a lacuna – ◡ ◡ – after ἀρχαιοπρεπῆ or – – ◡ ◡ before it. The lost word was probably a proper name, or may have continued the idea of πρόπασα χώρα, or have been in antithesis to θνατοί in 430.—ξυνομαιμόνων, the Titans.

427 f. ἔποικον ἕδος 'Ασίας νέμονται, lit. *inhabit the settled abode of Asia,* cf. Il. 4. 406 Θήβης ἕδος, &c. The phrase need not be pressed as a reference to the Greek colonies in Asia Minor,—an anachronism, as the schol. points out.

432. παρθένοι, the Amazons, for whom v. 749 ff. As Aeschylus places them in Europe, τε in 431 must mean *and,* not *both.*—μάχας is gen. with ἄτρεστοι, the usual construction with adjectives compounded with a- privative.

433. Σκύθης, v. 2 n.

436. 'Αραβίας: it is surprising to find Arabia near the Caucasus, which Aeschylus puts N. of the Euxine, v. note on 743. His geography is however so confused that it seems unnecessary to suspect the text, as many edd. do.

437 f. πόλισμα Καυκάσου πέλας: no passage identifying this place is quoted from the ancient geographers.

439 f. ὀξυπρώροισι compares the line of spears advanced to a naval squadron ready for the ἐμβολή (Tucker, *Supplices,* p. ix.).—ἐν αἰχμαῖς, *with,* cf. Eur. El. 321 καὶ σκῆπτρ' ἐν οἷς "Ελλησιν ἐστρατηλάτει.

441—6. The MSS. reading, as given in the text, may be construed *One other Titan-god alone ere now have I beheld in agony, subdued by adamantine chains of torment, Atlas, who ever groans beneath an overpowering mighty force and the vault of heaven upon his back.* But the text is probably corrupt: (1) ἀδαμαντοδέτοις λύμαις has occurred at 155 of Prometheus; it is less appropriate to Atlas, who could only metaphorically be said to be chained; and it renders ἐν πόνοις superfluous. It looks like an interpolation here, together with Τιτᾶνα, a gloss on θεόν. (2) ὑποστενάζειν, elsewhere *to groan low,* may here mean *groan beneath,* like ὑποστεναχίζω, but can hardly be trans. (3) σθένος does not elsewhere mean *strain* or *weight.*—No suggested emendation however is sufficiently certain to receive into the text.

447 ff. Cf. Sept. 883 (900) διήκει δὲ καὶ πόλιν στόνος, | στένουσι πύργοι, | στένει πέδον φίλανδρον. ξυμπίτνων, *in unison,* falling in with (his groans),—or with (the calling of the sea), if we put the comma after κλύδων.—ὑποβρέμει suggests 'rumbles a bass': cf. 128 n.—Ἄϊδος μυχὸς γᾶς : the latter words form a single idea, *cavern*; cf. Eur. Supp. 53 τάφων χώματα γαίας.

454. *προυσελούμενον : v. LS. Both the form and the derivation remain uncertain.

456. παντελῶς, *finally,* perhaps here means, as Wecklein explains it, *in the last resort*: the gods were assigned their various prerogatives by Zeus (245), but it was by aid of Prometheus that the new régime had been brought about (235).

457. αὐτά, emphatic, 'the prerogatives themselves': *but what these are I say not.*

458 ff. τὰν βροτοῖς πήματα is explained by ὥς σφας νηπίους κ.τ.λ. : *the former miseries of men, and how they were as babes until I made them wise*: cf. 99 n.

461 f. *Nor shall I speak as having any reproach against mankind* (i.e. as holding them to blame for their former helplessness), *but to set forth the benevolence of my gifts.*

463 ff. πρῶτα μέν, *aforetime,* as though τέλος δὲ ἐγὼ κ.τ.λ. followed at 473; not *in the first place,* taken up by ἦν δ᾽ οὐδέν 470, since βλέποντες—εἰκῆ πάντα is not the first of the series of miseries, but a general description of the whole.

465. τὸν μακρὸν βίον, during the full term of life, i.e. *all their life long,* cf. 553.

466 f. οὔτε...οὐ, cf. 495 f.

468. ἀήσυροι occurs elsewhere only in Ap. Rhod. 2. 1103 of Boreas gently stirring the leaves on the topmost boughs of trees; the word is explained by scholia as meaning there 'lightly blowing' (ἄω), and here 'easily moved by the wind,' and so light, *tiny.* If the word was associated with the rustling of leaves, it may perhaps here refer to the restless movements of ants and be represented by *busy.*

473 f. τὰς δυσκρίτους belongs in sense to ἀντολάς as much as to δύσεις: cf. 21 n.

475. καὶ μήν, *furthermore,* calling attention to a fresh point: cf. 1114 n.

476 f. γραμμάτων κ.τ.λ., *and the combining of letters, that record of all things, creative mother of the arts.* Mnemosyne is the mother of the Muses in Hes. Theog. 52. Ἐργάνη, *worker,* is elsewhere a title of Athena as goddess of women's industries and of the arts generally.

478. **κνώδαλα**, *brute beasts*, hitherto undomesticated; usually of wild animals.

479. **ζεύγλαισι δουλεύοντα** is proleptic (just as **φιληνίους** 481 means *taught to love the rein*). Parallel with it is **σώμασίν θ' ὅπως—γένοιντο**: *to be in bondage to the collar, and with their bodies to bear in men's stead their heaviest toils.* Hermann takes **σώμασίν τε** with **δουλεύοντα** of the bodies of *riders*, comparing **σωματηγός** and **σωματηγεῖν** used of saddle-animals; but **ἔζευξα ἐν ζυγοῖσι** indicates animals for draught.

486 f. **σόφισμ' ὅτῳ...ἀπαλλαγῶ**: for the 'interrogative' or 'deliberative' subj. in a dependent clause v. G. 1490.

488. **αἰκὲς πῆμα**, *an untoward disaster*, is explained by what follows : your cleverness has failed you in your own case.

489. **κακός**, *bad*, i.e. unskilful, cf. Cho. 773 (777) **κακός γε μάντις ἂν γνοίη τάδε**.

490 f. **σεαυτὸν...εὑρεῖν**, *in thine own case canst not find*; the subj. of the dependent verb is for emphasis put first as obj. of the main verb, though not logically its obj. as in the normal form of this idiom, v. 99 n. —**ἰάσιμος (εἶ)**: the 1st and 2nd persons of **εἰμί** are not usually omitted unless **ἐγώ** or **σύ** is expressed, as in 42, 191; here **σεαυτόν** does duty for **σύ**.

495 f. **οὔτε...οὐ...οὐδέ**, *neither...nor...nor yet*, cf. 466 f. **οὔτε...οὐ**, Hdt. 1. 138 **οὔτε...οὔτε...οὐ...οὐδέ**.

500—515. Prometheus claims to have taught the chief kinds of divination, viz. (1) **ὀνειροπολία**, the interpretation of dreams; (2) **οἰωνιστική**, *augurium, auspicium*, divination by the movements of birds, with which would be classed chance signs like **κληδόνες** and **σύμβολοι** (Ar. Av. 721 **φήμη γ' ὑμῖν ὄρνις ἐστί, πταρμόν τ' ὄρνιθα καλεῖτε, | ξύμβολον ὄρνιν**); (3) **ἱεροσκοπία**, *haruspicium*, divination from sacrifices, the principal signs noticed being the appearance of the intestines and especially of the gall and liver of the victim, and the nature of the flame with which it burnt. No mention is made of the important class of **διοσημεῖα**, thunder and lightning, eclipses, earthquakes &c., but as they were simply unlucky portents no doubt they did not need Prometheus to explain them.

501 f. *I first distinguished which among dreams should really come to pass*, or possibly *discerned from dreams what things should come to pass in reality.* The former rendering seems preferable, as it follows the common use of **κρίνειν ἐκ**, *to select from*; it recalls the Homeric classifi-

cation of dreams into two kinds, the true that came through the gate of horn and the false that came through the gate of ivory (Od. 19. 560 ff.). In either case the phrase is suggested by the idiomatic κρίνειν ἐνύπνιον, *to interpret a dream* : cf. ὀνειροκρίτης, *an interpreter of dreams,* and Cho. 37 κριταὶ δὲ τῶνδ' ὀνειράτων.—The pl. ἅ would show that ὕπαρ is adv. acc., not nom.

502 f. *Signs from chance words obscure I made known to them and signs from meetings by the way.* κληδών like its synonym φήμη denotes (1) as here, an omen conveyed by some casual utterance that can be taken to refer to the enterprise in hand : e.g. in Od. 20. 98—121 Odysseus overhears one of the women grinding at the mills pray for the destruction of the suitors, and accepts the omen as foretelling his success; (2) a rumour of mysterious origin, the Homeric ὄσσα, such as the report of the victory over the Persians at Plataea that on the same day miraculously passed through the Greek armament at Mycale, Hdt. 9. 100 f.—σύμ-βολος is an omen given by a chance meeting with a person. Wecklein quotes from Chrysostom, Hom. 12 on Ephes. ὁ δεῖνά μοι πρῶτος ἐνέτυχεν ἐξιόντι τῆς οἰκίας· πάντως μυρία δεῖ κακὰ συμπεσεῖν. From the schol. on Ar. Av. 722 συμβόλους ἐποίουν τοὺς πρῶτα συναντῶντας, the word appears to mean lit. *a person encountered* (συμβάλλεσθαι *to meet*), though doubt-less confused with σύμβολον *a token, sign* (συμβάλλειν *to interpret*). In Xen. Apol. 13 σύμβολοι are coupled with μάντεις, and there and in Mem. 1. 1. 3 appear in a list with οἰωνοί, so that LS. seem to be wrong in understanding οἰωνός with σύμβολος.

504 ff. πτῆσιν οἰωνῶν : it appears in Homer (Leaf on Il. 12. 239) that the interpretation might depend not only on (1) the position of the bird, right or left of the observer, but also (2) on the direction of its flight, to E. or W., the quarters of light and darkness, and (3) on attendant circumstances,—chief importance being attached to (3) when possible. Hence δεξιός easily passed into the sense of *propitious,* δεξιὸς φύσιν, whether on the right hand or left.—εὐώνυμος (like ἀριστερός if from ἄριστος) is a euphemistic name for the unlucky side : cf. εὐφρόνη, Εὐμενίδες, εὐλογία in mod. Gr. for φλογιὰς νόσος, *smallpox,* &c. and *meioses* like παθεῖν τι *to die.* Such euphemisms originated in the primitive belief that the mention of an evil can cause it to occur, a superstition that lingers in the form of a vague dislike of calling un-pleasant things by plain names.—δίαιταν, *habitat, haunt.*

510. εἴη πρὸς ἡδονήν, sc. τὰ σπλάγχνα, cf. 277 n.

511. This clause is in apposition with the two preceding ones, χολῆς λοβοῦ τε defining σπλάγχνων and ποικίλην εὐμορφίαν referring to χροιάν and λειότητα.

515. **ἐξωμμάτωσα, ἐπάργεμα** are transferred from the seer to the thing seen : *of fire-eyed signs, I purged the vision, over-filmed before* (Miss Swanwick).

516. **δή**, *so, then*, connecting, as 232.

517. **ἀνθρώποισιν** with **ὠφελήματα** : cf. 639 βροτοῖς δοτῆρα, and for ὠφελεῖν c. dat. cf. 358.

518. **ἄργυρον χρυσόν τε** coupled together form the third member of the enumeration : cf. Cic. de Div. 1. 116 aurum et argentum, aes, ferrum.

525 f. After hearing Prometheus the Chorus are convinced that he is wise enough to be able to procure his own release and reinstatement.

527 f. *Not thus as yet is consummating fate destined to bring these things to pass.* The personal construction **μοῖρα κρᾶναι πέπρωται** is substituted for the usual impersonal πέπρωται μοῖραν κρᾶναι: cf. δίκαιός εἰμι δρᾶν τι. Or possibly **κρᾶναι** is intrans., *to come to puss* (so Cho. ad fin.), in which case **ταῦτα** is its subject and **μοῖρα πέπρωται** stands for simply πέπρωται. In either case μοῖρα is not fully personified as in Homer, since in 532 Aesch. adopts the Hesiodic conception of the Fates as three.—In the following lines Prometheus again hints at the secret of his release, cf. 183 n.

529. **ὧδε** recapitulates the preceding participial clause, as often οὕτω δή. **φυγγάνω**, prophetic pres., v. 184 n.

532. **Μοῖραι τρίμορφοι**: the one name denotes three forms or persons, χ 226 πολλῶν ὀνομάτων μορφὴ μία.

534. **γε** marks assent, though the form of expression is modified : when pressed Prometheus drops the personification of the Fates and Furies and reverts to the stricter conception of destiny as impersonal, the necessity that is stronger than any personal will, even that of Zeus.

536. **οὐκέτι**, in its logical sense, 'when you come to that,' cf. 801.

540. **σῴζων**, *keeping secret.*

541. **ἐκφυγγάνω**, v. on 529 φυγγάνω.

543. **θεῖτο...ἀντίπαλον**, v. 174 n.

546. **ποτινισσομένα**: epic prep. and vb., cf. 123 n.

550 ff. **τόδε** is sometimes taken to refer to the aspiration just expressed, to be pious and humble : but the sentence implies rather some fresh maxim : viz. **ἡδύ τι κ.τ.λ.**, *'tis sweet to pass the whole life long*, &c. —**ἐκτακείη** may be a metaphor from melting away the writing on a wax tablet, as we say *to blot out of recollection*; so literally Ar. Nub. 772 πρὸς τὸν ἥλιον τὰ γράμματ' ἐκτήξαιμι. Cf. the metaphor at 815.—τὸν μακρὸν...βίον, cf. 465 n.

[Dr Verrall (*J. Hell. Stud.* 1. 264) is guided by the form ἡδύ (sic MSS, edd. ἀδύ) and the non-tragic words θαρσαλέος, φανός, ἀλδαίνειν, εὐφροσύνη, to discover in 552—5 an adaptation of an actual elegiac γνώμη—

ἡδύ τι θαρσαλέαις μακρὸν βίον ἐλπίσι τείνειν
φαναῖς τ' ἀλδαίνειν θυμὸν ἐν εὐφροσύναις—!

It may at all events be admitted that Aeschylus is imitating the style of the gnomic poets.]

557. After this line a line corresponding to 548 seems to have been lost: conjectures are Ζηνὸς κότῳ (Headlam), γυιοφθόροις, χαλκευμάτων.

559. †ἰδίᾳ γνώμᾳ, *in self-will*, so ἰδιογνώμων, *of independent mind*, Hippocrates, Aristotle; but the line does not correspond metrically with 550, and is probably corrupt.

561 ff. φέρ', ὅπως χάρις *ἁ χάρις, εἰπὲ κ.τ.λ. *Come say how thy boon is a boon to thee? where is there aid and what? what succour in the creatures of a day?* χάρις is hard to translate, as it combines the senses of the service rendered and the return expected for it. Cf. Forbes on Thuc. 1. 33: 'κατατίθεσθαι χάριν is (lit.) to "invest" an act of kindness in the hope of getting it repaid with interest.' For the order ὅπως...εἰπέ cf. Soph. Ant. 1190 ἀλλ' ὅστις ἦν ὁ μῦθος αὖθις εἴπατε: for ὅπως...ποῦ... cf. 631 f. ὅτι...τί...: usually when coupled together the direct interrog. pron. precedes the indirect (Jebb on Soph. O. T. 71).

566. ἰσόνειρον: cf. the epic ἴσος, ἰσόθεος, the latter occurring also in tragedy; Cho. 318 ἰσόμοιρον (unless M's ἰσοτίμοιρον points to ἀντίμοιρον as the correct reading there).

567. ἐμπεποδισμένον (ἐστί) = ἐμπεπόδισται.

569. τὰν Διὸς ἁρμονίαν: the expression is adopted from the Pythagoreans, who conceived the ordered universe symbolically as a musical harmony (Ar. Met. 1. 5).

573. The simple construction τὸ διαμφίδιον δέ μοι μέλος προσέπτα...ὅτε...ὑμεναίουν is broken by the insertion of τόδ' ἐκεῖνό τε: *then flew to my mind that strain unlike to this, when I sang...*

575. λουτρά, sc. νυμφικά. 'At Athens both bride and bridegroom washed on the wedding day in water fetched from the fountain Callirrhoë': Gardner and Jevons, *Greek Antiquities*, p. 345.

577. ἰότατι γάμων, *because of*, on the occasion of; in Homer the word is used only of persons, *by the will of*, passing into the sense of *for the sake of* or *because of* in some passages, e.g. Il. 15. 41, Od. 11. 384.

578. ὁμοπάτριον, sc. ἡμῖν: a schol. on Od. 10. 2 speaks of this Hesione as daughter of Oceanus.

579 f. [ἕδνοις], rejected to restore metrical correspondence with 569. Nor is the word strictly correct, for in Homer it denotes presents given by the bridegroom not to the bride but to her parents, a survival of the primitive custom of marriage by purchase (v. Leaf on Il. 9. 146). —ἄγαγες πιθών, *wooed and won*.

581. The story of Io is briefly told in the Supplices 297 (291) ff. She was the daughter of Inachus king of Argos, where she was a priestess of Hera. Zeus fell in love with her, whereupon Hera transformed her into a heifer, and when Zeus changed himself into a bull, put her under the charge of the myriad-eyed Argus. Argus was killed by Hermes (hence, as was supposed, called Ἀργειφόντης). Hera then sent a gadfly (οἶστρ.s, μύωψ) to drive Io away. Maddened by its sting she fled from land to land, and in her wanderings has now reached the place where Prometheus is bound.—She enters calmly, but at 587 is distracted by a fresh attack of madness; in it she passes from wild raving to a passionate prayer to Zeus (600), subsiding into a piteous appeal (612 f.), which Prometheus answers as addressed to himself. Her attention is again attracted, and after one or two recurring spasms (624, 9) her madness disappears. At the end of the scene (903) a fresh outburst of frenzy carries her away from the spot.

583. χειμαζόμενον, perhaps literally *storm-beaten*, rather than as often metaphorically *distressed*; at 864 it is metaphorical.

584. ποινάς, *as a penalty*, acc. in apposition with the sentence, like 641 δίκην (G. 915).

588. οἶστρος in spite of the vague τις may be taken literally, not metaphorically *frenzy*.

589 f. Stung to madness by the gadfly, Io fancies that Argus though dead still haunts her—a dramatic touch, which would be spoilt by taking the εἴδωλον as an objective ghost (some editors even suppose that it was represented on the stage). εἴδωλον Ἄργου may be construed as an exclamation, or as object of εἰσορῶσα and in apposition with βούταν: ἄλευ', ἆ Δᾶ being parenthetical, *keep him away, O Earth* (or *Zeus*, v. LS. δᾶ).

596 f. ὑποτοβεῖ, cf. 128 n. νόμον, cogn. acc.—κηρόπλαστος δόναξ, *wax-moulded reed*, i.e. a σύριγξ or Pan's pipe, a row of reeds of graduated length fastened together with wax, upon which Argus as a cowherd had played, and the sound of which Io still hears in the buzzing of the gadfly.

600 ff. The order of the words is τί ποτε ἁμαρτοῦσάν με εὑρὼν ἐνέζευξας ἐν ταῖσδε πημοναῖς;

603 f. οἰστρηλάτῳ δείματι, for *the terror of the gadfly's pursuit*, is like 155 ἀδαμαντοδέτοις λύμαις. The dat. goes with παράκοπον τείρεις, *torturest to frenzy*.

610. γεγυμνάκασιν, *have exercised*: the metaphor is in 616 f. re-inforced by the cogn. acc. δρόμους γυμνάζεται.

623 ff. κέντροις φοιταλέοις: the epithet is transferred from Io herself, as in νήστισιν αἰκίαις.—σκιρτημάτων αἰκίαις, poetic apposi-tional gen. like Homer's τέλος θανάτοιο: *leaping in torments of hunger, wildly rushing I come, the victim of Hera's vengeful arts*.

631 f. ὅ τι...τί, cf. 561 ff. n. ὅπως...ποῦ.

639. βροτοῖς δοτῆρα, cf. 517 ἀνθρώποισιν ὠφελήματα.

641. δίκην: for the acc. cf. 584 n.

648. ἀρκῶ...σαφηνίσαι: *Thus much alone can I avail to tell thee.* ἀρκῶ c. inf., *I am enough to=can*, occurs also Pind. Ol. 9. 1 τὸ μὲν 'Αρχιλόχου μέλος...ἀρκεσε...ἀγεμονεῦσαι, *sufficed, was good enough to lead*. Here the inf. makes the refusal less brusque than it would be with the part. σαφηνίσας, *It is enough for me to tell thee*, the usual construction.

649 f. καί...γε, cf. 73 n.—It seems preferable to construe τέρμα as obj. of δεῖξον, further defined by the dependent interrogative τίς... χρόνος, rather than to take τέρμα as predicate to ἔσται.

654. τί...μέλλεις μὴ οὐ: τί μέλλεις is equivalent to μὴ μέλλε, and μέλλειν itself contains an idea of negation; both these negatives are idiomatically repeated with the dependent inf.; cf. 251 f. n., 813, 950, 1089; G. 1617.—γεγωνίσκειν, v. 209 n.

656. μᾶσσον ὡς: ὡς=*than* after comparatives is probably to be accepted in a few instances, e.g. Xenophanes fr. 3. 4 οὐ μείους ὥς περ χίλιοι εἰς ἐπίπαν, Plato Rep. 7. 526 c μεῖζω...ὡς τοῦτο, Apol. 36 D with Adam's note. [It has been proposed less well to take ὡς ἐμοὶ γλυκύ separately from μᾶσσον, *care for me no more,—as is my pleasure*.]

657. ἄκουε δή, *so listen*, cf. 57 n.

660. πολυφθόρους, *hazardous*, is specially applied to the dangers of travel; cf. 846 τῆς πολυφθόρου πλάνης, Soph. fr. 499 οἱ ποντοναῦται... οἱ πολύφθοροι. So also φθείρεσθαι is used of the hardships of a voyage Eur. Hel. 774, or of shipwreck, v. LS.

663. κασιγνήταις πατρός (οὔσαις): Oceanus was the father of the rivers (Hes. Theog. 337): the father of Io was Inachus, the river and king of Argos.

665. ὅπου μέλλοι: the opt. is regularly used in a conditional or indefinite relative clause, depending on a modal verb or verbal phrase and an inf., which together are equivalent to an opt. with ἄν: **τἀπο-κλαῦσαι ἀξίαν τριβὴν ἔχει**=οὐκ ἂν μάτην ἀποκλαῦσαι τις. Cf. Eum. 728 (725) οὐκοῦν δίκαιον τὸν σέβοντ᾽ εὐεργετεῖν, | ἄλλως τε πάντως χὥτε δεόμενος τύχοι. M. and T. 502, 555.

667. Note the absence of caesura : cf. 6 n.

670 f. **διαφθορὰν...ὅθεν προσέπτατο**, cf. 99 n.

672. **γάρ** introduces a promised narrative, as at 855.—**πωλεύμεναι**: for the Ionic form cf. 123 n.

677. **τέθαλπται**, cf. 615: the word is chosen with reference to **ἱμέρου** rather than to **βέλει**, being like θερμαίνω and other synonyms regularly used of love, hope, anger, ℥ emotions such as fear and despair that send a chill (κρύος) to the heart.

679. **Λέρνη**, the marsh on the coast S. of Argos, famous as the abode of the Hydra.

682. **εὐφρόνας** : for the word see on εὐώνυμος 506.

685. **ἔς τε Πυθὼ κἀπὶ Δωδώνης** : the variation of the preposition (cf. 855 f., 1060 f.) is doubtless only metri gratia ; ἐπί c. gen. properly denotes the direction rather than the point reached.

691. **ἐπισκήπτουσα** communicates to **μυθουμένη** the sense of *commanding*, c. inf. : cf. 347 n., 1096 n.

693. **ἄφετον** is specially applied to consecrated cattle that wandered untethered in the precincts of a temple, and so foreshadows Io's transformation, as do 678 ἀπολακτίσῃς and 680 βουστάσεις.—**δλᾶσθαι**, inf. of purpose, common after vbs. of *sending* and the like, G. 1532.

694. **πυρωτόν,** *fiery*, cf. fr. 300 (304) πυρωτὸν φλόγα.—**μολεῖν** : the aor. inf. is used in a future sense after vbs. signifying *to give an oracular response*, on the analogy of vbs. of *commanding* or *warning*: cf. Il. 13. 666 πολλάκι γάρ οἱ ἔειπε...νούσῳ ὑπ᾽ ἀργαλέῃ φθίσθαι...ἤ...ὑπὸ Τρώεσσι δαμῆναι (M. and T. 98).

700—9. Cf. 581 n. Io simply states what happened, accepting events and not asking who caused them.

708 f. **οἰστροπλὴξ μάστιγι θείᾳ**=οἴστρῳ, μάστιγι θείᾳ, πλησσομένη.

709. **γῆν πρὸ γῆς** : in this idiom **γῆν** is the poetic acc. of the goal of motion, while **πρό** is local, *to one land in front of*, i.e., *after another*.

714—721. This short ode is structurally useful to make a break in a long scene (636—902), while dramatically it serves to emphasize the cruelty of Io's fate : her story has worked upon the feelings of the Ocean-nymphs until they burst into an almost hysterical cry of horror.

726 ff. **τὴν πρίν γε—ἐξηγουμένης** is logically subordinate to **τὰ λοιπὰ νῦν ἀκούσατε.**

728. **τὸν ἀμφ᾽ ἑαυτῆς ἄθλον,** i.e. ἐξηγουμένης τὸν ἑαυτῆς ἄθλον or ἐξηγουμένης ἀμφὶ (περὶ) ἑαυτῆς. Cf. the common idiom with verbs of motion, e.g. Thuc. 2. 80. 1 ἀδυνάτων ὄντων ξυμβοηθεῖν τῶν ἀπὸ θαλάσσης 'Ακαρνάνων for τῶν παρὰ θαλάσσῃ 'Ακαρνάνων or τῶν 'Ακαρνάνων ἀπὸ θαλάσσης ξυμβοηθεῖν.

732. **θυμῷ βαλέ,** cf. Soph. O. T. 975 ἐς θυμὸν βαλεῖν, and for the local dat. 288 n., Sept. 1039 (1048) κινδύνῳ βαλεῖν and the Homeric ἐνὶ φρεσὶ βάλλεο σῇσιν.

734. **στρέψασα σαυτήν:** Io has come N.E. from the Ionic gulf (864), and is now to turn E. or S.E. (see on 739).—**στεῖχε...γύας,** cf. 863 κέλευθον ἦξας, Sept. 453 (466) κλίμακος προσαμβάσεις στείχει.—**ἀνηρότους,** because the Nomad Scythians were a pastoral people, ζῶντες μὴ ἀπ᾽ ἀρότου ἀλλ᾽ ἀπὸ κτηνέων (Hdt. 4. 46). Herodotus (4. 19) places them N. of the Euxine and E. of the River Panticapes.

735. **Σκύθας ἀφίξῃ:** for the poetic acc. of the goal of motion cf. 709, 743, 756, 761, 834.—**πλεκτὰς στέγας,** i.e. of wicker-work, covered with felt according to Strabo 7. 307 αἱ σκηναὶ πιλωταὶ πεπήγασιν ἐπὶ ταῖς ἀμάξαις: cf. Hor. Od. 3. 24. 9 campestres...Scythae quorum plaustra uagas rite trahunt domos.

738 f. **πελάζειν, ἐκπερᾶν,** inf. for imper., G. 1536.

739. **ῥαχίαισιν:** is this the coast of the Ocean or of the Euxine? If the former, Io is to start eastward from the scene of the play and keep along the shore of the Ocean till she has passed the region of the Nomads, and then apparently to turn south away from the coast (this is not stated), so as to leave the Chalybes on the left. If the Euxine be meant, Io starts south-east (πρὸς ἀντολάς in 733 might bear this sense from the extreme north) striking straight across to the Euxine, and keeps to its coast past the Nomads and the Chalybes: **λαιᾶς χειρός** then applying to the former as much as to the latter. Neither interpretation is without difficulty, and Aeschylus can hardly have had a clear idea of the route in his mind.

740. **λαιᾶς χειρός:** the gen. of place within which, or on the side of which, is mostly poetic, but in this phrase occurs also in Hdt. and Attic inscriptions, e.g. δεξιᾶς εἰσιόντι, *on the right as you enter.* G. 1137. —The Chalybes were the earliest workers in iron known to the Greeks (who got most of their iron ware from people at a lower level of civilization). Hence Χάλυψ is used for *steel,* as at 137. They lived in the N. of Asia Minor, where the Ten Thousand encountered a warlike tribe

of them in the mountains of Armenia and another detachment living by working iron in Pontus near the coast (Xen. Anab. 4. 7. 15, 5. 5. 1). Aeschylus transfers them to Scythia, as the Scythians were also known as metal workers. Hence he speaks of the scene of the play as σιδηρο-μήτορα αἶαν 317, and calls iron Σκύθης and Χάλυβος Σκυθῶν ἄποικος (*this Chalyb from distant Scythia*) Sept. 802, 715 (817, 727).

743. Ὑβρίστην is probably to be thus written as a proper name, though it does not occur elsewhere; for though ὑβριστήν could stand as an adj. (cf. Hes. Theog. 307 δεινόν θ' ὑβριστήν τ' ἄνεμον), yet Aeschylus would hardly write *the violent river, true to its name*, and leave us to guess what the name was. Aeschylus obviously places the Caucasus N. of the Euxine and W. of the Lacus Maeotis. The Hybristes rises in the Caucasus, but in the uncertainty of Io's route at this point we can hardly infer whether it runs N. into the Ocean or S. into the Euxine. It seems idle to try to identify it with the Hypanis or any actual river. It may be classed with the River Pluto and Papyrus Mountains (832,7), names that Aeschylus perhaps invented himself.

744. εὔβατος περᾶν, a pleonasm like 792 ῥητὸν αὐδᾶσθαι.

745. πρὸς αὐτὸν Καύκασον, i.e. to the very source of the river.

749 ff. This country of the Amazons we learn from 431 to be Colchis, which Aesch. therefore correctly places S. of the Caucasus but transports with that mountain into Scythia. The Amazons' migration Herodotus (4. 110) reverses, making a section of them leave the Thermodon in Pontus for the neighbourhood of the Lacus Maeotis.

752 f. Salmydessus was really nowhere near the Thermodon, being the name of the W. coast of the Euxine from the mouth of the Thracian Bosporus to the promontory of Thynias. Ships were often wrecked on its shallows, and the crews were then plundered by the natives (Strabo 319, Xen. Anab. 7. 5. 12 ff.). Hence the Black Sea got its name of Ἄξενος (Εὔξεινος later by a euphemism, cf. 506 εὐωνύμους n.), echoed here in ἐχθρόξενος.—γνάθος: the Schol. explains that the sea here had the form of an ass's jaw; no doubt the word may be intended both to describe the configuration of the coast and to imply that it swallowed up ships.

755 f. ἰσθμόν, the Tauric Chersonese (Crimea); λίμνης, the Lacus Maeotis (Sea of Azof); αὐλῶνα Μαιωτικόν, its outlet, the Cimmerian Bosporus (Straits of Kertch).—θρασυσπλάγχνως, i.e. plunge boldly in and swim across.

759 ff. Βόσπορος: the traditional derivation here alluded to, βοὸς πόρος, is open to the objection that no other word shows the stem of βοῦς in composition as βοσ-. The word is explained as a dialectical

form of φωσφόρος, a title of the moon-goddess Hecate, worshipped at the Thracian Bosporus, whence the name was transferred to the Cimmerian (Wecklein). Io was associated with both channels, and in the Supplices is made to cross the former.—Herodotus (4. 45) mentions that some people make the Cimmerian Bosporus and the Tanais the boundary between Europe and Asia, others the Phasis in Colchis. Aeschylus adopted the latter in the Prometheus Solutus, fr. 191.

771. **λοιπὸν τῇδε**, *remaining for her.*

774. **τί** does duty first as *what* and then as *why.*—**ἔρριψα**: the aor. is idiomatically used with **τί οὐκ**, expressing surprise that the deed is not already done ; with the 2nd pers. it amounts to an exhortation to do it (M. and T. 62). Cf. the 'instantaneous' aor., 194 n.

775 f. **ὅπως…ἀπηλλάγην**, cf. 166 n.—**πέδοι**, cf. 288 n.

779 ff. **θανεῖν μέν**, as though followed by τέρμα δὲ μόχθων οὐδέν ἐστι προκείμενον ; instead of which after the parenthesis **αὕτη γάρ**… **ἀπαλλαγή**, there follows **νῦν δέ**, *but as it is*, as though preceded by εἰ μὲν θανεῖν πεπρωμένον ἦν, αὕτη ἦν ἂν πημάτων ἀπαλλαγή.

782. **πρὶν ἂν Ζεὺς ἐκπέσῃ**: at 274 Prometheus replied to the Chorus in a humbler tone, πλὴν ὅταν κείνῳ δοκῇ : here indignation at Io's sufferings makes him speak more bitterly. He reverts to the secret that he has twice already hinted to the Chorus (180 ff., 527 ff.), and now in part reveals it.

786. **ὡς…ὄντων τῶνδε μανθάνειν**, lit. *in the belief that this is so, you may learn (it)*, the gen. abs. replacing the object of the verb, ὄντα (or ὡς ὄντα) τάδε μανθάνειν. This idiom occurs also in prose: G. 1593. It is seen developing in phrases like Eur. Bacch. 792 οὐ δέσμιος φυγὼν σώσει τόδε ; *Remember thine escape from bondage.*

788. Cf. 19 n., and for the order 953, Ag. 827 (836) τοῖς αὐτὸς αὐτοῦ πήμασιν.

790. **ἀσχαλᾷ**: for the form cf. 171 n., for the prophetic pres. 184 n., 793, and in a dependent clause 227.—For the marriage here foretold, cf. 954 ff. n., and v. pp. xvi f.

792. **τί δ' (ἐρωτᾷς) ὅντινα (γάμον γαμεῖ);—ῥητὸν αὐδᾶσθαι** (mid.), cf. 744, Ar. Av. 1713 οὐ φατὸν λέγειν.

796. **ἂν…λυθείς**, sc. ἀποστροφὴ ἂν εἴην, i. e. εἰ λυθείην, ἀποστρέψαιμ' ἂν τὴν τύχην.

797. **ὁ λύσων**, the potential use of the fut. part., cf. 27 ὁ λωφήσων. —**ακοντος Διός**: ἐκών and ἄκων are used as participles, G. 1571.

798. **τῶν σῶν τιν' αὐτῶν ἐκγόνων**, *one of thy very descendants*, almost equivalent to σῶν αὐτῆς, *thine own descendants.* Prometheus was

to be liberated by Heracles (897 ff.), Io's descendant in the thirteenth generation, but not against the will of Zeus (cf. 274), so that this reply ignores the words ἄκοντος Διός in the question.

801. οὐκέτι, logical: at this point the prophecy becomes hard to interpret; cf. 536. Io's perplexity is not without cause: Prometheus has foretold (1) that Zeus shall fall, (2) that his own release may avert this, and (3) that this release will be effected; but has not definitely stated that the last prophecy cancels the first; on the contrary, he keeps the prospect of Zeus's overthrow still before his mind, and foretells it again at 990, though in reality it never came to pass.

802. καὶ μηδὲ σαυτῆς γε..., *Ay, and not thine own fate either* : cf. Soph. O. C. 1432 καὶ μή μ' ἐπίσχῃς γε, *yea—and detain me not*.

806 f. ἑλοῦ γάρ· ἢ...φράσω...ἢ... Some edd. write ἑλοῦ γὰρ ἢ..., assuming a survival of the Homeric ἢ...ἤ, *whether...or*, in a dependent question. But probably the few cases in tragedy should be corrected either by making the question independent, as here, or by altering the former ἤ to εἰ (Jebb on O. C. 80, Verrall on Cho. 889).

808. τούτοιν (τοῖν χαρίτοιν), fem., G. 410.

809. μηδ' ἀτιμάσῃς λόγου sc. νώ, understood from τῇδε and ἐμοί above: cf. Soph. O. C. 49 μή μ' ἀτιμάσῃς...ὧν σε προστρέπω φράσαι.

810 ff. γέγωνε, γεγωνεῖν, v. 209 n.—τὸ μὴ οὔ, v. 251 n., 654 n.

816. Io's journey is resumed from 761, so that the ῥεῖθρον is the Cimmerian Bosporus. Continuing eastward from this, she is to arrive finally at Aethiopia and the Nile (833 ff.): the mythical regions she traverses on the way seem therefore to be placed vaguely on the eastern confines of the world, from north to south. [Some commentators have supposed her to go round by the north of Europe (visiting the Arimaspi there) to the *west*, through Spain and across the sea to the Gorgons in Libya (see on 819), and so to Aethiopia. Decisive objections to this route are (1) it makes her double back across her line of travel from the scene of the play to the Bosporus (733—761), and (2) she is described as coming to the Gorgons (819) before the Arimaspi (831).]—The sentence has no main verb, and in default of any convincing emendation we may suppose a line or more lost after 817.

818. πόντου, possibly the Caspian. Apparently Io is to swim across, as across the Bosporus 755 f. n.

819. The daughters of Phorcus (or Phorcys), the Graeae with their one eye and one tooth between them, and the Gorgons with snakes for hair, are familiar from the story of Perseus. Hesiod (Theog. 274) speaks of them as πέρην κλυτοῦ Ὠκεανοῖο, ἐσχατιῇ πρὸς νυκτός (cf. Homer's πρὸς

EXPLANATORY NOTES.

ζόφον of the west (χ πρὸς ἠῶ τ' ἠέλιόν τε); later writers put them in Libya. A schol. on Pind. Pyth. 10. 72 however mentions that they were also thought to be in the south-east. Aeschylus seems to place them in the east, though still making them dwell in darkness (822 f.).— **Κισθήνης**: a fr. of Cratinus, κάνθένδ', ἐπὶ τέρματα γῆς ἥξεις καὶ Κισθήνης ὄρος ὄψει may be a parody of this passage. The historical Cisthene was a town in Mysia.

820 f. **δηναιαὶ κόραι** refers to their name Γραῖαι, *old women.* Their resemblance to swans is not elsewhere mentioned.

827. **φρούριον** can hardly mean *precaution*, and even less *thing to guard against*, the sense given by scholia and required by the context (cf. 741, 830). Perhaps *guard-post, fort*, of the region held by the Gorgons, cf. Cic. *Tusc.* 2. 10, translating *P. Sol.*, Transverberatus *castrum hoc Furiarum* incolo (Margaret E. Hirst, *C. Rev.* XXXVI. p. 18).

829 ff. About the griffins and the tribe that stole the gold they guarded, see Hdt. 3. 116, 4. 13 and 27. They were described, says Herodotus (expressing incredulity), by Aristeas of Proconnesus, who wrote an epic called Arimaspea about his travels among the north-eastern tribes; and the name Ἀριμασποί was from the Scythian ἄριμα *one* and σποῦ *eye*. Aeschylus had doubtless read the Arimaspea. As he mentions the Arimaspi between the Gorgons and the Aethiopians, he appears to put them in the east rather than the north-east or north. Ctesias, Indica 12 (circ. 400 B.C.), transfers the griffins and the gold to India, but does not mention the Arimaspi. The griffin, a winged lion with an eagle's head, was perhaps borrowed by Greek art from the Semitic east: the name γρῦψ is identical with *cherub*, Hebrew *krûb* (Frazer's *Pausanias* II. p. 319).—**ἀκραγεῖς**, *not barking* (κράζω), qualifies the metaphor **κύνας** (used of servants or guardians of the gods, v. LS.), to show that they are not real hounds: so the eagle is Διὸς πτηνὸς κύων 1054, the winged horse is a τετρασκελὴς οἰωνός 411, and the gadfly's sting is ἀρδις ἄπυρος 905; cf. Cho. 491 (493) πέδαις ἀχαλκεύτοις of the robe in which Agamemnon was entangled.

832. **νᾶμα Πλούτωνος πόρου**, *the stream of the river Pluto* (cf. Eum 293 Τρίτωνος ἀμφὶ χεῦμα...πόρου) is not mentioned elsewhere, and may be an invention of the poet, like the river Hybristes 743. The name is intended to suggest πλοῦτος: it was applied to Hades as god of the earth and so giver of its wealth of minerals and fruits.

833. **τηλουρὸν δὲ γῆς**, *on the confines of the earth*, partitive gen. with the local adj. as with adverbs like ποῦ, πόρρω &c.; cf. 1 χθονὸς... τηλουρὸν πέδον, 872 ἐσχάτη χθονός.

834 f. ἡλίου πηγαῖς, *the source of the sun,* the east, as Soph. fr. 655 *νυκτὸς πηγάς* of the west; cf. 109 *πυρὸς πηγήν.* The phrase may be suggested by the name of the sacred spring at the temple of Ammon, *ἡλίου κρήνη* (Hdt. 4. 181).—The early Greeks conceived the Aethiopians as covering the whole of the south of the world, as the Scythians the north (Strabo 33).

835 ff. ποταμὸς Αἰθίοψ, here only, appears to be the Nile above its *καταβασμός,* i.e. the First (northernmost) Cataract: Solinus 32 states that above this point the Nile was called Nigris (Niger=Αἰθίοψ). For the belief that the Nile rose in the E. cf. Strabo 696: Alexander finding crocodiles in the Hydaspes (Indus) thought he had discovered the source of the Nile. The name Αἰθίοψ (associated with αἴθω and ὄψ, but perhaps like *Niger* really a native word) is transferred from the κελαινὸν φῦλον to their river, as though it too were sunburnt.—**Βιβλίνων ὁρῶν,** *the Papyrus Mountains,* appears to be another fiction of the poet; cf. 832 n.—**Νεῖλος,** *as Nile.*

839. τὴν τρίγωνον χθόνα, *τὸ καλεόμενον Δέλτα,* Hdt. 2. 13.

840. μακράν, *distant.*

846. γεγωνεῖν, v. 209 n.—**πολυφθόρου,** v. 660 n.—**πλάνης,** *about her wandering,* an objective gen. with τι: so with an interrog. pron. e.g. Soph. El. 317 *τοῦ κασιγνήτου τί φής;* [That the gen. does not depend in some way on the vb. is shown by its only occurring where the vb. has an object, whereas the vb. may be omitted, Eum. 211 *τί γὰρ γυναικὸς ἥτις ἄνδρα νοσφίσῃ;*]

849. τὸ πᾶν πορείας τέρμα, i.e. *τὴν πᾶσαν πορείαν ἐς τὸ τέρμα,* cf. 300 *τέρμα κελεύθου διαμειψάμενος.*

850. μάτην, *falsely,* cf. Eur. Ion 275 *ἆρ' ἀληθές, ἢ μάτην λόγος;*

853 f. ὄχλον τὸν πλεῖστον λόγων, *the chief bulk of the tale,* i.e. Io's route between Lerna (704) and Dodona (856), presumably by the Isthmus of Corinth: ἣ **αὐτὸ τέρμα,** the last part of her wanderings hitherto.

855 f. γάρ, cf. 672 n.—**γάπεδα,** *plains:* for the Doric form cf. *γάμορος, γάποτος* &c.—For **πρὸς...ἀμφί,** cf. 685 n., 1060 f.; for **ἀμφί,** *to the neighbourhood of,* cf. 1061.

858. αἱ προσήγοροι δρύες: the rustling of the leaves of these sacred oaks was regarded as the voice of the god and was interpreted by priestesses to enquirers who consulted the oracle (see for a full account Jebb's *Trachiniae,* Appendix ad fin.).

861. τῶνδε προσσαίνει σέ τι; *does aught of this appeal to thee?* i.e. does it awake memories, do I tell it rightly?

863. κόλπον 'Ρέας, the Ionian sea or Adriatic, called by Apollonius Rhodius (4. 327) Κρονίην ἅλα.

864. *Whence on a backward-roaming course thou art driven* (like a ship in a storm): i.e. north-eastward, to the scene of the play[1]. χειμάζῃ, cf. 583 n.; pres., because the journey is not yet finished.

866. Ἰόνιος (ῐ), but Ἰω (ῑ): the southern part of the Adriatic was so named from the Ionian colonies on Cephallenia and the other 'Ionian Islands.'

867. μνῆμα, acc. in apposition with the sentence, expressing purpose, as Ag. 234 (224) ἔτλα θυτὴρ γενέσθαι θυγατρός, πολέμων ἀρωγάν. G. 915.

871. τῶν πάλαι λόγων, 841; πάλαι often denotes the quite recent past.

872. Κάνωβος gave its name to the westernmost branch of the Nile, higher up which was the Milesian colony of Naucratis, the only trading port in Egypt open to foreigners in early times (Hdt. 2. 178).—ἐσχάτη χθονός, *the farthest point of land* at the mouth of the river.

874. τίθησι prophetic pres.—ἔμφρονα: Aeschylus nowhere says that Io's form was restored by Zeus as well as her senses.

[1] Io's route has been given in four sections, and may now be summarized:—

(703—9.) Driven from Argos she fled to Cerchnea and Lerna and thence wandering from land to land

(855—867.) she came [presumably by way of the Isthmus of Corinth] to Molossis and Dodona, and to the Gulf of Rhea, henceforward called the Ionian Sea. Thence she reversed her course [and reached the scene of the play, near the Ocean in the far north].

(733—761.) On departing she is to go east past the Nomad Scythians and Chalybes to the river Hybristes, ascend it to its source in the Caucasus [which Aeschylus places north of the Euxine], and crossing that mountain go south through the country of the Amazons to the Cimmerian Bosporus, which she will cross from Europe into Asia.

(816—840.) [At this point we pass from erratic geography into a region more purely mythical. The route appears to traverse the far east from north to south.] Entering Asia Io is to keep eastward, crossing the sea [? the Caspian] to the plains of Cisthene, the home of the Graeae and Gorgons, avoid the griffins and Arimaspi by the banks of the Pluto, and reach the dark race that dwells at the confines of the earth near the springs of the sun, on the river Aethiops. This she will descend, past the cataract in the Bibline mountains, where it becomes the Nile, and so reach the Delta.

See further the notes *ad loca* above. It may be remarked that Io's wanderings as recounted in the Supplices, 547 (538) ff., follow an entirely different course: there she roams from the meadows of Argos through many lands, crosses the *Thracian* Bosporus, and traverses Asia Minor and Phoenicia to Egypt. [Io's route has been fully discussed by Hermann in his edition of Aeschylus, II. 152 ff., and by B. Foss in the pamphlet referred to on p. xxiv.]

875. ἐπαφῶν (ἐπαφᾶν for ἐφαφᾶν, ἀφάω, ἀφή): the word is associated with the miraculous birth of Epaphus, καὶ Ζεὺς ἐφάπτωρ χειρὶ φιτύει γόνον Supp. 316 (312); cf. Mosch. 1. 50 Ζεὺς...ἐπαφώμενος ἠρέμα χερσὶν πόρτιος Ἰναχίης, and ἐφάπτωρ, ἔφαψις, ἐπαφή Supp. *passim.* —**ἀταρβεῖ**, 'fear-less,' i. e. *causing no fear* (so ἄφοβος 932), according to the schol.; and this is more appropriate than the usual meaning *feeling no fear*, as merely a stock epithet of Zeus.

According to Herodotus (2. 153, 3. 27 f.) *Epaphus* is the Greek form [a sort of reduplication possibly suggested by the word ἐπαφᾶν] of *Apis*, the name of the Egyptian bull-god. The story of healing by touch and generation ἐξ ἐπαφῆς κἀξ ἐπιπνοίας, θείαις ἐπιπνοίαις Supp. 17, 584 (18, 576), is oriental in character, and perhaps was an accretion to the Io legend borrowed from Egypt. Io herself was identified with Isis.

876. γεννημάτων, unless corrupt, must mean γεννήσεως.

877. κελαινόν, being a native of Egypt.—**καρπώσεται**, as king.

879. πέμπτη...γέννα: Epaphus — Libye — Belus — Danaus — the Danaids.—Danaus with his fifty daughters fled from Egypt to Argos in order to escape from the sons of his twin-brother Aegyptus. These followed and demanded the Danaids in marriage. Finally Danaus pretended to consent, but gave to each of his daughters a dagger, with which they killed their husbands on the bridal night. Lynceus alone was spared by Hypermnestra, succeeded to the throne of Argos, and was the ancestor of Heracles (897 f.). Cf. Hor. Od. 3. 11. 30 ff.— The arrival of Danaus and his daughters at Argos and their protection by the king Pelasgus against their pursuers form the subject of the Supplices of Aeschylus, which is almost certainly the first play of a trilogy.

882. ἐπτοημένοι (ἔρωτι), as often.

883. λελειμμένοι, *outstripped,* c. gen. of comparison, as νικᾶσθαι, ἡττᾶσθαι.

885. φθόνον ἕξει (= φθονήσει) **σωμάτων** (τῶν παρθένων αὐτοῖς), *God shall deny them their brides.*

886 f. *And the land of Pelasgus shall receive them—when vanquished and slain by women's boldness in the watches of the night.* **δέξεται** (αὐτούς), **δαμέντων** (αὐτων): cf. Soph. Trach. 803 τοσαῦτ' ἐπισκήψαντος, ἐν μέσῳ σκάφει θέντες σφε..., Eur. Hel. 58 ξὺν ἀνδρί, γνοντός...*with my husband, when he knows.* The irregularity is specially harsh here, and it would be better to understand (αὐτάς) as obj. of **δέξεται**, *shall welcome the maids, when their wooers have been slain,* were it not that the Danaids have been welcomed at Argos before they slay their cousins.

With the former interpretation, ll. 886—9 explain 885, φθόνον δὲ σωμάτων κ.τ.λ., and δέξεται is ironical: the land they hoped would receive them, received their dead bodies.—θηλυκτόνῳ, cf. Eur. I. T. 1083 πατροκτόνος χείρ, a father's murderous hand.—Ἄρει δαμέντων... θράσει: the dat. of the agent (G. 1186 f.), common with δαμῆναι in Homer, is reinforced by the instr. dat.: cf. for the double dat. 55 f.— νυκτιφρουρήτῳ, watching by night, from φρουρέω intr., act. like νυκτι- πλαγκτός and 949 πιστός; or possibly waiting for the night, cf. Eur. Alc. 27 φρουρῶν τόδ᾽ ἦμαρ, and for the form πανδλωτος all-capturing, πάμφθαρτος all-destroying.

891 f.   παίδων ἵμερος, desire for children.   τὸ μὴ κτεῖναι, cf. 251 n.

896.   The asyndeton and the repetition in 901 f. are remarkable. Prometheus checks his prophecy abruptly.

897.   *σπόρος in the sense of offspring, son, is not found elsewhere in tragedy, but occurs frequently in Lycophron, the constant imitator of tragic usage (Sikes and Willson).—γε μήν, yet, resumptive; possibly a contrast is intended between θρασύς and ἄναλκις 894.—Cf. 798 n., 879 n.

901.   ὅπως δὲ χώπῃ (ταῦτα γενήσεται), cf. 947.

903.   A fresh attack of madness, represented in language of in- creasing wildness, drives Io from the scene.—ἐλελεῦ, on! properly a battle-cry.

904 f.   ὑποθάλπουσι, either inwardly or gradually inflame, begin to inflame.—φρενοπληγές may be either act. like ἀμφιπλήξ or pass. like οἰστροπλήξ.

906.   ἄπυρος, not forged in fire, explains that ἄρδις is metaphorical; cf. n. on 829 ff. ἀκραγεῖς κύνας.

907.   φρένα, cf. 377 n.

908.   Metaphor follows metaphor kaleidoscopically: τροχοδινεῖται seems to suggest ἔξω δρόμου φέρομαι, a phrase properly used of a racing chariot, cf. Cho. 1020 (1022) ὥσπερ ξὺν ἵπποις ἡνιοστροφῶ δρόμου | ἐξω- τέρω of incipient madness; though πνεύματι and the following lines imply rather a ship driven out of her course.   θολεροί, turbid, like the stormy sea; but in the rest of the sentence Io's λόγοι are imagined not as the waves but as the vessel that they buffet: cf. Sept. 194 (210) νεὼς καμούσης ποντίῳ πρὸς κύματι: πταίουσι (cf. 958) is regularly used of a ship striking on a rock. [Paley sees in the last lines a metaphor 'de- rived from the muddy waters of a river battling with the clear waves at the aestuary,' but 'the waves of madness' would surely not be clear.]

913 ff.   ὃς πρῶτος ἐν γνώμᾳ κ.τ.λ.: maxims in this sense are ascribed to Cleobulus and to Pittacus.

919 ff. τῶν...διαθρυπτομένων, τῶν...μεγαλυνομένων, objective gen. after γάμων.

930. ἀλατείαις πόνων, for the adjectival gen. cf. 226 n. and Eur. Bacch. 1218 μόχθων μυρίοις ζητήμασι.

932 ff. ἄφοβος *without fear,* in the sense of causing no fear, cf. Plat. Legg. 797 A λόγον οὐκ ἄφοβον εἰπεῖν, and 875 n. ἀταρβεῖ.—μηδὲ must be taken as *but...not,* δέ answering μέν above; so οὐδέ in Homer. —κρεισσόνων θεῶν, where a human maiden would say κρεισσόνων ἀνδρῶν.—[ἔρως] ἄφυκτον ὄμμα προσδράκοι με: edd. explain ὄμμα as cogn. acc., which would only be possible if it could have the meaning of δέργμα, but for this no parallels are quoted. We are forced to take it in apposition with ἔρως, *never may the love of the greater gods, never may their all-seeing eye look upon me* (schol. μηδὲ ἐπίδοι με ὁ ἔρως κρεισσόνων θεῶν, ὃς ἐστιν ἄφυκτον ὄμμα). But more probably ἔρως is to be omitted as an interpolated gloss.

935.   *That war were no war, and its resources but resourcelessness.* ἄπορα πόριμος, lit. *providing difficulties,* the verbal adj. with an object in the acc., as Soph. Ant. 786 σὲ φύξιμος.

940. οἷον=ὅτι τοῖον, v. LS.

941. αὐτόν *himself,* in his turn, as he ousted his father ; cf. 374,6 n.

942. πατρὸς ἀρά : no reference to this occurs elsewhere.

947. ᾧ τρόπῳ, sc. ἐκτροπὴ γενήσεται, cf. 901.

948 f. κτύποις πιστός=πεποιθώς, cf. 817 νυκτιφρουρήτῳ n.

950 f. τὸ μὴ οὐ πεσεῖν, cf. 251 n., 654 n.

952. τοῖον παλαιστήν, the παῖδα φέρτερον πατρός 794, that is to be the fruit of Zeus's marriage.

953. ἐπ' αὐτὸς αὐτῷ, cf. 788 n.

954 ff. This is a reminiscence of Pindar Isthm. 7. 27 ff., where it is said that Zeus and Poseidon were suitors for Thetis, but relinquished her when Themis foretold that she should bear a son stronger than his sire, ὃς κεραυνοῦ τε κρέσσον ἄλλο βέλος διώξει χερὶ τριόδοντός τ' ἀμαιμακέτου. Aeschylus, regardless of the fact that in adapting the myth to the story of Prometheus (v. pp. xvi. f.) he has omitted Poseidon's wooing, retains the reference to his trident here for its impressiveness.

955. ὑπερβάλλοντα, c. gen. like ὑπερφέρειν and other verbs of comparison.

956 f. *And the sea's earthshaking pest, Poseidon's trident spear, shall shatter.* τινάκτειραν νόσον suggests *palsy.* (The masc. τινακτήρ is not found; Soph. Trach. 502 has Ποσειδάωνα τινάκτορα γαίας.)—σκεδᾷ:

no exact parallel for this use is quoted; we have in Homer λαὸν σκέδασεν, *routed*, and 25 πάχνην σκεδᾷ.

960. I.e., in your prophecy, the wish is father to the thought.

961. πρός, adverb.

967. δ' οὖν, with imper., impatient and contemptuous, *well then, let him do it;* cf. Eum. 226 σὺ δ' οὖν δίωκε—καὶ πόνον πλέω τίθου.—ποιείτω; like τοῦτο ποιεῖν in prose, is used instead of repeating the preceding verb.

968. *'Tis wise to bow to her from whom there is no escape*, i.e. to speak humbly. Adrasteia was a personification of the divine wrath excited by proud speech, and was identified with Nemesis. Προσκυνῶ τὴν Ἀδράστειαν or Νέμεσιν (Plato), σὺν δ' Ἀδραστείᾳ λέγω (Eur.), were formulae of apology for words that sounded presumptuous. Adrasteia was probably in origin a Phrygian goddess, the name being either Asiatic or a Greek translation of an Asiatic word (Roscher, *Lexikon*). Greek grammarians derived it from ἄδραστος (διδράσκω), in the sense of ἀναπόδραστος, ἄφυκτος.

969. *Worship, pray, court the conqueror of the hour:* for the form cf. 408.

970. ἔλασσον ἤ μηδέν, cf. Plat. Theaet. 180 A ἧττον αὐτοῖς ἔνι (c. inf.) ἤ τὸ μηδέν: μηδέν expressing abstract nothingness usually has the art. ; but cf. Soph. El. 1000, κἀπὶ μηδὲν ἔρχεται.

972. ἄρξει θεοῖς : for the dat. cf. 49 n.

987. νέον νέοι κρατεῖτε, cf. 35 : *young are ye and your empire.*—δή lays stress on δοκεῖτε, *you fancy*, much as it often marks a quotation of another's opinion, v. 13 n.

989. δισσοὺς τυράννους, Uranus and Cronus.

990. ἐπόψομαι, *shall live to see*, v. LS. s.v. ἐπεῖδον. For the prophecy v. 801 n.

993. πολλοῦ γε καὶ τοῦ παντὸς ἐλλείπω, *From that I am far, nay altogether removed*, lit. *I fall short of much, or rather of all (of it)*, cf. 1038 τοῦ παντὸς δέω and the common πολλοῦ γε καὶ δεῖ: ἐλλείπειν takes a gen. of the thing in which deficiency exists, the degree of deficiency being usually expressed by an adverbial acc., as in 357, but here by an adj. of quantity.

997. κατούρισας, lit. *hast brought into port with a favouring wind*, as we say, 'have landed yourself in.'

1000 f. are assigned with most edd. to Hermes, οἶμαι being ironical and λατρεύειν πέτρᾳ a retort to λατρείας in 998. L. 1002 may be taken either as justifying this insulting word, or as deprecating Hermes' rudeness as unprovoked—*such insolence should be kept for the insolent.* The MSS. give 998—1002 all to Prometheus, and it is certainly possible to obtain a sense from this reading: *At all events I would not exchange my troubles for your servitude. Better, methinks, to serve this rock than to be father Zeus's trusty messenger,—so to repay your insolence in kind.*

1009 f. νόσον (cogn. acc.) = μανίαν, as 400 f. and often: *Thy words reveal thee sore diseased with madness.—Mad I may be, if...*

1014. καὶ μήν, *and yet,* γε emphasizing σύ, *thou for one.* Cf. 1017, Ag. 1253 (1254).

1015. γαρ, (*True*) *for* (*otherwise*)...

1017. *Yet should I owe him a favour, I would pay it,* i.e. I do not owe him such a favour yet.

1018. ἐκερτόμησας: the aor. referring to the words just spoken as already past (cf. 1098) is akin to that in 194.—δῆθεν, cf. 218 n.: *Thou mockest me then.*

1026. κυκάτω καὶ ταρασσέτω, sc. Ζεύς, cf. 1084,6.

1030. δή may be taken in the sense of καὶ δή (cf. 57 n.), with ὦπται, which replies to ὅρα, rather than as emphasizing πάλαι, which means *already, from the first,* not *long, long ago.*

1033. ὀχλεῖς is probably absolute, μάτην με going with παρηγορῶν.

1038. τοῦ παντὸς δέω, lit. *I lack the whole of it,* sc. τοῦ οὕτω ποιεῖν.

1039. πολλὰ καὶ μάτην, cf. Eum. 144 ἦ πολλὰ δὴ παθοῦσα καὶ μάτην ἐγώ. Lit. *It seems that I shall speak saying much and to no purpose,* i.e. If I say what I intend (the ultimatum beginning at 1047), it will be a long tale told in vain.

1041. ἐμαῖς emphatic, 'mine at all events.'

1046. οὐδενὸς μεῖζον σθένει, lit. *is stronger than nothing else,* i.e. *is the weakest of all things;* cf. Theognis 411 οὐδενὸς ἀνθρώπων κακίων, *best of men,* Eur. Andr. 726 τἄλλ' ὄντες ἴστε μηδενὸς βελτίονες, and οὐχ ἥκιστα, *most of all.*

1048. κακῶν goes in sense with χειμών as well as with τρικυμία, cf. 21 n.

1049. ἔπεισ' ἄφυκτος: the elision of -ι in the personal termination -σι is rare.

1054. πτηνὸς κύων, cf. 829 n.

1055. σώματος...ῥάκος: the gen. is one of definition, 'your rag of a body,' while ῥάκος is 'proleptic,' expressing the result of the vb.: *shall rend thy huge body all to shreds.*

1056. πανήμερος, *the whole day long;* according to fr. 193 (preserved in Cicero's translation, Tusc. 2. 24) the eagle came *tertio quoque die*, every other day.

1059 ff. **πρὶν ἄν θεῶν τις κ.τ.λ.** Hermes reports Zeus's condition doubtless thinking it impossible, but it was eventually fulfilled, v. p. xvi.

1060 f. **εἰς...ἀμφί,** cf. 685 n. **ἀμφί,** *to the region of*, cf. 856.

1063. **καὶ λίαν εἰρημένος** is explained by Wecklein as meaning *only too expressly stated*. But it is doubtful whether the words could bear this sense; nor does λίαν mean *very, verily* in the sense of *truly* (LS). Sikes and Willson translate *only too definitely uttered*. But, as the next l. shows, the question is not whether Zeus did or did not say it, but whether he said it truly. Probably **εἰρημένος** is a corruption for **ἐτήτυμος** (Hartung) or **ἀληθινός,** the whole being a regular rhetorical formula, cf. Plato Rep. 485 E **μὴ πεπλασμένως ἀλλ' ἀληθῶς,** Deinarch. 99. 35 **οὐ γὰρ ψεῦδός ἐστιν ἀλλὰ καὶ λίαν ἀληθές** (Headlam in *Cl. Rev.* XII. 189).

1068. **ἡμῖν μέν,** without a corresponding δέ, as often μέν with a personal pronoun.

1074. **οὐδὲν ἀεικές** probably has its usual sense, *is nothing strange*, carrying on the idea of **εἰδότι τοι μοι κ.τ.λ.,** rather than *is no disgrace*, repudiating **αἰσχρόν** in 1071.

1079. **αὐταῖς ῥίζαις,** cf. 237 n.—**πνεῦμα,** *the blast*, meaning 'the confined vapour in the interior of the earth, to which upheavals of the ocean-bed, and consequently vast and destructive waves, are attributed. Strabo (6. 258) uses both **πνεῦμα** and **ἄνεμος** in this sense, in speculating on the disruption of Sicily from Italy' (Paley).

1081 ff. The subj. of **συγχώσειεν** is **πνεῦμα,** that of **ῥίψεις** and **θανατώσει** (Ζεύς), cf. 1026.

1086. Cf. 965.

1089. **μὴ <οὐ>,** cf. 251 n., 654 n.

1090. **χαλᾷ** (ὅδε), intrans.

1091. **ἀλλ' οὖν,** 'but at all events,' cf. 1104.

1096 f. *Suggest and urge me to some other course, whereto thou mayst persuade me.* **ἄλλο τι** is common to both vbs., and so practically is **με,** though **φώνει** alone would require a dat.: cf. 691 n.—**καὶ πείσεις,** (not only advise but) also persuade.

1098. **παρέσυρας,** v. LS.; the metaphor is not clear: elsewhere the word means *to sweep along, carry away* something, of a river in flood, a hawk swooping &c.; here perhaps the idea is that of trailing a bait or net (so σύρω) *past* the victim, παρα- possibly having the additional connotation of leading *astray:—for never, never will I descend to* *that to which thou lurest me.* This interpretation adds point to the metaphors from hunting in Hermes' reply, 1105, 1112.

1103. **ἀπέπτυσα**: the 'instantaneous' aor. (v. 194 n.) is common with this verb.

1109. **αὐταὶ δ' ὑμᾶς αὐτάς**, sc. εἰσεβάλετε.

1114. **καὶ μήν**, *lo now!* calling attention to a fresh occurrence, as often to the entrance of a person on the stage; cf. 475 n.—For the question of the representation of the storm v. p. xxvi.

1116. **βρυχία**, *from the depth*, probably connected with βρέχω (*rigo, Regen, rain*), but like ὑποβρύχιος not confined to the sense of *under water*.—**παραμυκᾶται**, *rolls roaring.*

1121. **ἀντίπνουν**: the lengthening of a short vowel that receives the ictus before the liquids λ μ ν preceded by a mute is in tragedy usually confined to the case of soft mutes, β γ δ.

1122. I.e. the waves touch the sky.

1123 f. **φανερῶς** refers to ἐπ' ἐμοὶ Διόθεν τεύχουσα φόβον, *'Tis aimed at me—from Zeus 'tis manifest this turmoil cometh to affright me.*

1125. **ὦ μητρὸς ἐμῆς σέβας**=ὦ σεβαστὴ μῆτερ, as we say 'your majesty'; i.e. Ge Themis (cf. 225 n.). Prometheus appeals to Earth and Air as together making up the universe, cf. 88 ff., Soph. O.C. 1654 γῆν τε προσκυνοῦνθ' ἅμα καὶ τὸν θεῶν Ὄλυμπον, Eur. Med. 57 γῇ τε κοὐρανῷ λέξαι. [A less probable interpretation is to take σέβας in apposition with **αἰθήρ**, *Aether, adored of my mother*,—in reference to the marriage of Aether (or Uranus) and Earth, for which v. fr. 44, Virg. Geor. 2. 325, &c.—Paley, who inclines to reject the identification of Ge and Themis at 225, sees here a natural appeal to Themis as a witness against injustice.]

CRITICAL NOTES.

The present text is constructed mainly from the materials provided by Wecklein's Berlin edition of Aeschylus (1885—93), which contains Vitelli's collation of the Medicean MS and a complete collection of the conjectural emendations of previous scholars. For the readings of the later MSS Wecklein must be supplemented by Dindorf (1841—51) and Hermann (1852).

The *Prometheus Vinctus* presents little serious textual difficulty, although a number of small points are open to question. The following notes deal with the more important. In presenting the MSS evidence Wecklein's notation is employed as follows:—

M the Codex Mediceus, an 11th century MS in the Laurentian Library at Florence. Besides the seven plays of Aeschylus it contains the tragedies of Sophocles and the Argonautica of Apollonius Rhodius. (For Sophocles it is usually quoted as Laurentianus or L. See the Introduction to Jebb's *Sophocles*, 1897.)

m a second hand that has corrected M's text of Aeschylus, apparently in part by conjecture, but mainly from comparison with the original from which M was copied; it has added interlinear glosses, and scholia in the margin.

m¹ two or three later hands, which may be classed together, that have added corrections and scholia of less value.

rec. one of the later MSS;

recc. several or all of them. Of the eight 13—15th century MSS described by Wecklein, six contain the *Prometheus Vinctus*.

M is the most correct as well as the oldest MS of Aeschylus. After its paramount value had been pointed out by Elmsley, there was a tendency to regard all the other copies as derived from it: thus Wecklein (vol. I. p. viii.) follows Cobet and Dindorf in believing that 'all the good readings of the other MSS are to be traced to the successful conjectures of grammarians, inasmuch as there is none that could not be discovered any day by any grammarian of moderate erudition.' It is doubtful however whether this can be maintained in certain passages (e.g. P. V. 20, 448, 536, 732, 977, 982, where the variants from M do not look like conjectures): it is therefore probably safer to 'assume a common source for the Medicean and the rest than a filiation of the rest to the Medicean' (see Tucker, *Supplices* pp. xxvii. f.). In any case, the general correctness of M, though making it the basis of the text, does not seem sufficient to support its readings when intrinsically inferior : while in some places they are unquestionably wrong.   Trifling and generally accepted corrections are passed over in these notes, but about 30 places are mentioned where the readings of one or more of the later MSS have been preferred, and about 60 where conjectural emendations have been adopted.   The more important of the latter have been indicated in the text by the usual marks, thus:—

[ ] rejected as an interpolation,

< > inserted by conjecture,

* otherwise emended;

also † a corrupt passage not emended.

2. ἄβατον recc., ἄβατόν τ' M (which inserts τε also in 202, 726). An early variant is indicated by scholia on Il. 14. 78 and Ar. Ran. 814, which quote ἄβροτον εἰς ἐρημίαν.

6.   Restored from schol. Ar. Ran. 814; ἀδαμαντίναις πέδῃσιν ἐν ἀρρήκτοις πέτραις M, recc. (some omit ἐν): πέτραις apparently from 4.

20.   πάγῳ recc., τόπῳ M, [a gloss to distinguish the word here from πάγος *frost*: cf. e.g. Ag. 347 (336) τῶν ὑπαιθρίων πάγων, schol. ἢ τῶν ψυχρῶν λέγει παγετῶν ἢ τῶν ὀρεινῶν τόπων τῶν ὑπὸ τὸν αἰθέρα ὄντων. Headlam.]

28.   ἐπηύρου Elmsley, ἐπηύρω M, ἀπηύρω recc.   Some edd. retain ἐπηύρω, since ἐπηυράμην occurs in Aristotle, but for earlier Attic it is probably wise to keep to the correct forms, ἐπηυρόμην (2nd aor.) from ἐπαυρέω, ἀπηυράμην (1st) from (ἀπαυράω).

42.   γε rec., τε M, which is just possible in view of the fact that ἀεί qualifies θράσους πλέως as well as νηλής: cf. the common misplacement of τε with prepositions, e.g. Sept. 30 ἔς τ' ἐπάλξεις καὶ πύλας. But M errs over γε also at 77, 264 and 802.

49.   ἐπαχθῆ Stanley; ἐπράχθη MSS, retained by Dindorf, who translates *Omnia facta* i.e. *permissa nobis sunt praeterquam diis imperare* (comparing for the form, though not the sense, Eum. 125 τί σοι πέπρακται

πρᾶγμα πλὴν τεύχειν κακά;). But ἐπράχθη can hardly mean more than *All is achieved*, i.e. *all is ours* (or *thine*), *save to rule the gods*, and this does not suit the context.

51. Hartung conjectures with much probability ἔγνωκα· τοῖσδέ γ' οὐδέν.... The MS reading gives a sentence of unusual form, and, if τοῖσδε be taken to refer to the fetters, conflicts with l. 54, which appears to call attention to them for the first time.

54. ψάλια: ψέλια rec.

55. βαλών Stanley, cf. 71; λαβών MSS, but ἀμφὶ χερσὶν can hardly go with θεῖνε to mean *rivet them round his arms*.

66. ὑπὲρ στένω Weil (ὕπερ Pauw), ὑπερστένω m, recc. (which Paley retains, cf. ὑπεραλγῶ and ὑπερμαχῶ c. gen.), ὑποστένω M. Wecklein writes ὑπὸ στένω, but though στένω ὑπὸ (ἐμῶν) πόνων might stand, ὑπὸ σῶν πόνων may be doubted.

77. γε m¹, recc., σε M.

99. πῇ Turnebus; ποῖ MSS, which might possibly be justified by the idea of motion in ἐπιτείλαι.

112. τοιῶνδε recc., τοιάσδε M, which Hermann and Paley retain. But even if the words could stand for τοιάσδε ποινὰς (τοιῶνδε) ἀμπλακημάτων, τοιάσδε is not wanted, the qualification of ποινὰς τίνω being given by the next line.

113. ὑπαίθριος MSS, ὑπαιθρίοις Bloomfield, edd. But cf. Th. 1. 134. ι ἵνα μὴ ὑπαίθριος ταλαιπωροίη, Plat. Symp. 203 D ὑπαίθριος κοιμώμενος.

δεσμοῖς πεπασσαλευμένος C. G. Haupt, δεσμοῖσι πεπασσαλευμένος Robortelli; δεσμοῖσι πασσαλευμένος M, πασσαλευτὸς recc.; πασσαλευτὸς ὤν Turnebus, προυσελούμενος Wecklein (v. 454), προσπεπαρμένος Dindorf. M elsewhere adds -ι to the dat. pl. against metre.

118. τερμόνιον ἵκετ' Headlam, restoring the iambic metre, ci. Ag. 1076=1081 (1091=1096), Sept. 142=150 (157=165); ἵκετο τερμόνιον MSS, but the metre ≍‿‿‿‿‿‿‿‿‿‿ (for ἵκετο cf. 140 expl. n.)—whether dochmiac followed by paeon or vice versa—is unusual.

148. σκοπέλοισιν Headlam, cf. 4, 15, 20, 56, 154; σκοπέλοις ἐν MSS.

153. εἰσιδοῦσαν Hermann, εἰσίδουσα (with the termination blurred) M, εἰσιδοῦσιν, εἰσιδούσᾳ recc.

159. ἀθέτως (from Hesych. ἀθέτως· ἀθέσμως, οὐ συγκατατεθειμένως. Αἴσχυλος, Πρ. Δ.) Bentley: ἀθέσμως MSS, a gloss.

164. ἀγρίοις M, ἀγρίως recc.

165. μήτε Turnebus, μήποτε MSS, but this requires μηδέ instead of the following μήτε, nor could θεός be a monosyllable after ‿‿.

194 (=172). ἐρέθισε Turnebus, ἠρέθισε MSS.

196 (=174). δ' Porson, γὰρ MSS.

197 (=175). πᾷ. Turnebus, ὅπᾳ MSS.

202. καὶ recc., τε καὶ M : cf. 2.

203. [Ζεύς· ἀλλ'] rejected by Bothe metri gratia.

229. ὑπερσχόντας Porson, ὑπερεχόντας (sic) MSS.

233. προσλαβόντι M, recc., προσλαβόντα recc.

239. ἐξημείψατο M, recc., ἀντημείψατο recc.

262. καὶ μὴν MSS, ἦ μὴν Headlam, καὶ μὴ φίλοις (even for enemies) Mitschenko.

264. θνητούς γ' recc., θνητούς τ' M, recc., θνητοὺς recc.   Hermann θνητούς γε παύσας here and κατοικίσας in 266, as more idiomatic.

271—3 the MSS assign to the Chorus.   Welcker first gave 272 to Prometheus, who then takes out of the mouth of the Chorus the word αἰκίζεται (for τε we should perhaps with O. Ribbeck read γε, v. 42 n.), and adds κοὐδαμῇ χαλᾷ κακῶν, which suggests the further question οὐδ' ἔστιν ἄθλου τέρμα... (It must be noted however that such interruptions are usually not replies but questions, which the first speaker answers by completing his interrupted sentence: e.g. Pers. 737 (735), Soph. Aj. 109.)

280 f. τὸν κακῶς πράσσοντ' Stanley, τοὺς κακῶς πράσσοντας MSS.

283. θνητοῖς M, θνητοῖς δ' recc.

329. ὄχλον Doederlein, χόλον MSS; χόλον μόχθων naturally means anger at labours, obj. gen. (so schol. rec. τὴν λύπην τῶν νῦν δυστυχιῶν); but it is doubtful whether the words will bear the interpretation thy present anger at thy woes, i.e. the woes that cause thy present anger, shall seem to thee but sport. We should expect χόλον to mean the wrath of Zeus ; assuming this, Wecklein explains μόχθων as a gen. of quality (cf. 226, 930, and Eur. Bacch. 1218 μόχθων μυρίοις ζητήμασιν), in the sense of toil-causing ; but if this construction were possible, it should rather mean toilsome to Zeus himself. Paley takes μόχθων with παιδιάν, a mere mockery of trouble, but gives no parallel for such a use of παιδιά.

347. πάντων μετασχών: Weil, to avoid the inconsistency with 250, conjectures πόνων μετασχεῖν, Wecklein τούτων μετασχεῖν, for even having dared to share my troubles, i.e. even for sympathizing (without being actively guilty). But καί should then precede πόνων or τούτων μετασχεῖν.

349. πείσεις recc., πείθεις M, assimilated to the following εὐπιθής (εὐπειθής M).

359. θέλεις M : θέλοις recc., perhaps rightly—for the mixed con-

ditional construction cf. Soph. O. T. 851 εἰ...ἐκτρέποιτο,...φανεῖ, M. and T. 499.

363—388 are given by m¹ and recc. to Oceanus (in which case κασιγνήτου would mean *your brother*); but 363 connects with what precedes, and the whole leads on to 389 ff. This fine descriptive passage, though not specially appropriate to Prometheus, would naturally be assigned to the protagonist.

370. πᾶσιν δs MSS, unmetrical; εἷς δs Weil, θεὸs δs Headlam, πᾶσιν being a likely interpolation. Sikes and Willson omit δs, but the asyndeton is improbable.

387. θερμοῖs rec., θερμῆs M, recc.—ἀπλάτου Schuetz (cf. Pind. Pyth. 1. 21 ἀπλάτου πυρόs and v. expl. n. on 367) : ἀπλήστου MSS, a common confusion, cf. 742.

394. ὀργῆs: the line is quoted 6 times by Plutarch and others with ψυχῆs νοσούσηs.

415 f. δακρυσίστακτον [δ']: Heath restored the metre by rejecting δέ; Hermann also writes δ' εἰβομένα for λειβομένα (for the position of δέ cf. that of τε in Supp. 9).

416. ῥαδινὸν recc., ῥαδινῶν M, which with ὄσσων might mean *glancing*, but seems inappropriate of weeping eyes.

425. <θ' ἐσπέριοι> Wecklein, <τ' ἐσχατιαί> Weil, but τε after τε in 424, which connects the sentences, is unlikely.—στένουσι M, recc., στένουσα recc., a correction subsequent to the corruption. V. expl. n.

436. 'Αραβίας : 'Αβαρίας (the land of the Avars) Boissonade; 'Αρίας (the old name of the Medes, Hdt. 7. 62) Wecklein after Martin, suggesting that the ὑψίκρημνον πόλισμα is Ecbatana; the a of Ἄριος is elsewhere short, but Aesch. allows himself some licence in unfamiliar proper names.

437. ὑψίκρημνον [θ'] : Elmsley, following the schol., rejected τε as unmetrical, and probably due to an attempt to get over the geographical difficulty.

441—6. ἀδαμαντοδέτοις rec., ἀκαμαντοδέτοις (a *vox nihili*) M, recc.—θεόν M, θεῶν recc.—Ἄτλανθ' δs recc., Ἄτλανθ' ὡs M.—ὑπέροχον rec., ὑπείροχον M, recc.—Reasons for suspecting considerable corruption are given in the explanatory notes. A possible combination of suggested emendations is

μόνον δὴ πρόσθεν ἄλλον ἐν πόνοις
δαμέντ' ἐσειδόμαν θεῶν
Ἄτλαντος ὑπέροχον σθένος κραταιόν,

8—2

ὅς αἰὲν οὐράνιον πόλον
νώτοις ὑποστεγάζει.

Here the rejection of ἀδαμαντοδέτοις Τιτᾶνα λύμαις is Heimsoeth's (v. expl. n.). ῎Ατλαντος... σθένος, an epic periphrasis for ῎Ατλαντα, is Hermann's conjecture. With this αἰέν is not wanted, and it may have been transposed with ὅς from the following l. owing to the similarity of -ος and ὅς (Headlam); τε would then be interpolated to couple σθένος and οὐράνιον πόλον (Sikes and Willson). [Hermann less well leaves αἰέν with ὑπέροχον and inserts <ὅς γᾶν> οὐράνιόν τε πόλον: for this conception of Atlas v. 364 n.] ὑποστεγάζει, *upholds*, is Hermann's, στεγάζειν being equivalent to στέγειν which can bear that sense. [Wecklein <στέγων> ὑποστενάζει, keeping the latter to be echoed by στένει, στένουσι below, but this seems unnecessary.]

Hermann suggested that 441—451 was not an epode, but a third strophe and antistrophe; but this supposition presumes a hopeless amount of corruption; e.g. Heimsoeth to conform 441—6 with 447—51 reads

μόνον δὲ πρόσθεν ἐν πόνοις
εἰδόμαν θεῶν δαμέντ᾽
῎Ατλαντος ὑπέροχον σθένος κραταιόν,
<ὅς γᾶν> οὐράνιόν τε πόλον
νώτοις ὑποστεγάζει.

448. **βυθὸς** recc.; βαθύς M, when **βοᾷ** would be dat. with ξυμπίτνων, *falling in unison with his cries the ocean wave groans to its depth*: but the position and sense of **βοᾷ** are against this.

449. [δ'] rejected by Lachmann, both metri gratia and to keep up the asyndeton.

454. **προυσελούμενον** Askew, προσηλούμενον M, recc., προσελούμενον m, recc.

477. **μνήμην** M; μνήμην θ' m¹, recc., but Aeschylus is not likely to have attributed to Prometheus the invention of a *memoria technica*, such as is said to have been devised by his contemporary Simonides.— **ἐργάνην**, so quoted by Stobaeus; ἐργαν* M, ἐργάτιν m¹, recc., ἐργάτην recc.

479. **σώμασιν**: Pauw conjectures σάγμασιν, *pack-saddles*, with δουλεύοντα, but 478 indicates draught-animals.

481. **ἄρμα τ'** rec.; ἄρματ' M, recc., making σώμασίν θ' ὅπως— γένοιντο above go with this clause; but μεγίστων διάδοχοι μοχθημάτων applies to oxen or mules drawing ploughs or waggons, rather than to

horses, *the pride of vast wealth and luxury*, harnessed to chariots for war or racing.

495. **οὔτε** recc.; **οὐδὲ** M, but *οὐδέ…οὐδέ* mean *not even…nor yet.*

518. **σίδηρον** edd., *σίδαρον* M, *σίδηρόν τ'* recc.—**τε** recc., *δὲ* M.

536. **οὐκέτ' ἂν πύθοιο** recc., others *οὐκ ἂν πύθοιο*, one *οὐκ ἂν ἐκ·πύθοιο*: *οὐκ ἂν οὖν πύθοιο* M.

559. **ἰδίᾳ γνώμᾳ**, unmetrical, is probably a gloss that has ousted *αὐτοβουλίᾳ* (Heimsoeth): cf. Sept. 1044 (1053) *αὐτόβουλος ἴσθι*, schol. rec. *τουτέστι, τῇ ἰδίᾳ γνώμῃ ὃ βούλει πρᾶττε* (Headlam): *αὐτοβουλία* does not occur, but is formed like *ἀβουλία, εὐβουλία, ὀξυβουλία, ἑτεροβουλία.*

561. **φέρ', ὅπως χάρις ἁ χάρις** Headlam for *φέρ' ὅπως χάρις ἄχαρις* MSS. Edd. *ἄχαρις χάρις*, translating *come (see) how thankless was thy boon* (Sikes and Willson *φέρε, πῶς ἄχαρις χάρις ;*—to avoid the unparalleled construction of an indirect question depending on *φέρε*); but this would require either *ὡς ἄχαρις χάρις!* an exclamation, or *ὅπως (πῶς) οὐκ ἄχαρις χάρις ;*

567—9 (=577—9). **ἀλαὸν** < *δέδεται* > **γένος** Meineke (cf. Anth. Pal. 6. 296 *ἐκ γήρως ἀδρανίη δέδεται*), and *οὔπω* for **οὔποτε** Hermann. It seems preferable however with Lachmann to reject [**ἔδνοις**] in 579 (v. expl. n.): it may have crept in from the schol. on 580 *πείθων δάμαρτα· ἔδνοις πείθων τὴν ἐσομένην σοι δάμαρτα κοινόλεκτρον.*

580. **πιθὼν** m¹, recc.; *πείθων* M (cf. 349), which would mean *trying to persuade.* [The metre is not decisive, as the anacrusis is common, ≍ : ‒ ⏑ ‒ ⏑ ‒ ⏑ ‒ ‒.]

589. **ἄλευ', ἁ Δᾶ** M, *ἀλευάδα* recc.; *ἄλευ δᾶ* Schleussner, defending *ἄλευ* for *ἄλευε* by *παῦ παῦε* and *παῖ παῖε* in Aristophanes: these however are probably colloquial.—**φοβοῦμαι** most edd. omit as a gloss, leaving **εἰσορῶσα** to go with **χρίει με οἶστρος**= *οἰστροῦμαι*, cf. 216 ff.—These alterations would produce a line of the same metre as the preceding and following, *εἴδωλον Ἄργου γηγενοῦς—ἄλευ, Δᾶ.*

594. **κυναγετεῖ:** *κυναγεῖ* Hermann, to restore the dochmiac metre.

598 f. M has *ἰὼ ἰὼ ποῖ ποῖ' π'ὸ π'οι πο' π οἰ πῃ μ' ἄγουσι*, recc. some variant of this. Wecklein restores the metre by reading after Seidler and Meineke

> *ἰὼ ἰὼ πόποι,*
> *ποῖ μ' ἄγουσιν* < *πλάναι* >, *τηλέπλανοι πλάναι;*

comparing Sept. 124 (134) *ἐπίλυσιν φόνων, ἐπίλυσιν δίδου* for the repetition in dochmiac verse.

602 (=624). **πημοναῖς** rec., πημοναῖσιν M, recc. (cf. 113 n.); **πημο-σύναις** Hermann.

605 (=627). **<με>** Erfurdt, to correspond with 627.

612 f. given to the Chorus by the MSS, restored to Io by Elmsley.

624 (=602). **κέντροις <ἐὴ> φοιταλέοις** Sikes and Willson, scanning φοιταλέοις - ◡ - by synizesis; κέντροισι φοιταλέοισιν MSS, cf. 113 n.

626 (=604). **<"Ηρας>** Hermann; the schol. notes on 627 τοῖς τῆς "Ηρας.

632. **τί μῆχαρ ἢ τί** Martin, τί μὴ χρὴ MSS.

636. **ὅπερ** Etym. Magn., ὅτι M, recc., ὃ recc., cf. 848.

653. **τοῦδε τοῦ**: τοῦδέ σοι Turnebus.

669. **ὀδύρομαι**: M and most recc. add γρ. αἰσχύνομαι, which two have in the text.

684. **νυκτίφαντ'** M, νυκτίφοιτ' recc.—**ὀνείρατα** is possibly a corruption from 682 ὀνείρασιν: A. Nauck conjectures δείματα, Weil φάσματα.

694. **πυρωτὸν** M, πυρωπὸν recc., but **πυρωτός** is unobjectionable: it occurs in fr. 300 (304) and in a fr. of Antiphanes (R. Ellis in *J. Phil.* 41. 26).—πυρωπὸν ἂν Διὸς Elmsley, πυρῶπ' ἂν ἐκ Διὸς (πυρώψ=πυρωπός, cf. φλογώψ=φλογωπός) Sikes and Willson, εἰ μὴ θέλοι πυρωπὸν ἐκ Διὸς μολεῖν Naber; but v. expl. n.

704. **Λέρνης τε κρήνην** (Canter), or ἀκτήν τε Λέρνης (Bloomfield), seems a necessary correction for Λέρνης ἄκρην τε M, ἄκρον τε, ἄκραν τε, ἐς ἄκρην recc.; since there is no ἄκρα, whether hill or headland, at Lerna.

707. **ἀφνίδιος** (a form attested by Hesychius) Elmsley metri gratia, for αἰφνίδιος MSS (cf. ἄφνω, ἐξαίφνης). However the word does not occur elsewhere in poetry, and the tautology after **ἀπροσδόκητος** is suspicious. Headlam conjectures ἄπτερος (ἄπτερος, αἰφνίδιος...ἢ ταχύς Hesych.).

710. **ὅ τι** Turnebus, ἔτι MSS.

711. **πόνων** recc., πόνον M.

715. **<ὦδ'>**, Wecklein, is needed for the sense, for it could hardly be understood from 717.—ηὔχουν schol. and recc., ηὐχόμην M.

717. **καί** recc., om. M, recc.

719. **ψύξειν** olim Dindorf, ψύχειν MSS, but the fut. seems indispensable, and the corruption would be easy before **ψυχάν**.—[ἐμάν] omitted by most edd., metri gratia, as repeated from 716.

726. **χρείαν** recc., χρείαν τ' M, which could only be explained by saying that the corresponding καί with τὰ λοιπά 729 is lost because of the digression **μαθεῖν γάρ—ἐξηγουμένης**. But cf. 2 n.

732. βάλ' recc., μάθ' M, a gloss on the phrase θυμῷ βαλέ.

737. ἐξηρτυμένοι rec., ἐξηρτημένοι M, recc., but this requires τόξα, the 'retained' acc.

738. πόδας Turnebus; MSS γύποδας, apparently γυ- copied by error from 734 γύας and the correct πόδας added without erasure, when the whole was retained by later scribes as a proper name (schol. ἔθνος· τινὲς γυμνοπόδας): Hermann suggests as an alternative γυῖ' ἀλιστόνοις, πόδας being written over γυῖα as a gloss: but χρίμπτειν γυῖα, for πόδας, does not seem a likely phrase.

742. πρόσπλατοι Elmsley, πρόσπλαστοι MSS, cf. 387.

743. Ὑβρίστην Bothe (Ὑβριστήν Schuetz), ὑβριστὴν MSS, on which the schol. notes τὸν Ἀράξην, παρὰ τὸ ἀράσσειν καὶ ἠχεῖν τὰ κύματα αὐτοῦ. Ἀράξην Robortelli, and Eustathius states that Aesch. mentions the Massagetic Araxes and approves the derivation of its name from ἀράσσειν : but this may have been in a lost play.

748. ὑπερβαλοῦσαν present editor, ὑπερβάλλουσαν MSS.

786. μανθάνειν altered to μαθεῖν σοι, M (Sikes and Willson); μαθεῖν σοι recc., σοι μαθεῖν edd.

790. ἀσχαλᾷ: ἀσχαλεῖ Herwerden, as the prophetic pres. depending on the fut. γαμεῖ is doubtful.

798. αὐτῶν M, αὐτὸν recc.: Brunck αὐτῆς *one of thine own descendants.*

802. σαυτῆς γ' Hermann, σαυτῆς τ' M, σαυτῆς recc., cf. 42.

809. λόγου Elmsley: λόγους MSS, cf. Suppl. 383 (372) τάσδ' ἀτιμάσαι λιτάς, but the omission of τούσδε or ἐμούς would be impossible.

817 f. ἡλιοστιβεῖς: ἡλίου στιβεῖς (prophetic pres.) Pauw, στίβει (imper.) Hartung; but στιβέω, *to pace over,* occurs only in Soph. Aj. 874 πᾶν ἐστίβηται (pass.) πλευρὸν ἔσπερον νεῶν, and a verb denoting walking is inconsistent with πόντου περῶσα φλοῖσβον: where Heimsoeth accordingly conjectures παρεῖσα, *passing on one side,* but the word will hardly bear that sense. Keeping the Aeschylean ἡλιοστιβεῖς, Sikes and Willson conjecture πέρα σὺ for περῶσα, Headlam περᾶσαι (inf. for imper.) ; but either is unlikely with περάσῃς two lines above. We are reduced to supposing, with Heath, a lacuna after 817.

827. φρούριον MSS, φροίμιον Wakefield, but the story is nearly finished.

832. πόρου recc., πόρον M.

833. γῆς Headlam : γῆν MSS, an unlikely apposition with φῦλον : τηλουροῦ δὲ γῆς Wecklein.

837. Βιβλίνων M, Βυβλίνων recc. (βύβλος, βυβλίον are late forms of βίβλος, βιβλίον, Meisterhans, *Grammatik,* p. 22).

842. **τῶνδ'** Schuetz, τῶν δ' MSS, which some edd. retain, but the pronominal art. with δέ should be adversative.

848. **ἥνπερ** Hermann, ἥντιν' MSS, cf. 636.

855. **γάπεδα** Porson; δάπεδα MSS, as at Cho. 794 (798), with ᾱ, which Paley and Verrall defend as from δᾶ = γῆ, though elsewhere the α is short. Stephanus Byz. attests γάπεδον in trag., so it can hardly have been confined to the sense of *front garden*, which the grammarians (see Hermann *ad loc.*) assign to it.

876. **τῶν Διὸς γεννημάτων** (for which Wieseler plausibly conjectures γέννημ' ἀφῶν) would naturally be explained in the preceding line, which Heimsoeth alters to ἐπαφῶν τ' ἀταρβεῖ χειρὶ φιτύει γόνον, after Supp. 316 (312) καὶ Ζεύς γ' ἐφάπτωρ χειρὶ φιτύει γόνον. But the redundance of **καὶ θιγὼν μόνον** is natural to an etymological passage (for the change of tense, metri gratia, cf. 347 μετασχὼν καὶ τετολμηκώς: cf. also Cho. 5 κλύειν, ἀκοῦσαι). Hermann with more probability supposes a lacuna, and Sikes and Willson suggest <γόνου σε ποιεῖ διογενοῦς ἐγκύμονα> after **καὶ θιγὼν μόνον.** To explain the loss by *homoeoteleuton* it would be better to arrange thus (Headlam):—

> ἐνταῦθα δή σε Ζεὺς τίθησιν ἔμφρονα
> <γόνου δὲ ποιεῖ διογενοῦς ἐγκύμονα>
> ἐπαφῶν ἀταρβεῖ χειρὶ καὶ θιγὼν μόνον.

884. **θηρεύοντες** recc., θηρεύσοντες M, recc.; the pres. is perhaps more suitable, and the tragg. seem to prefer θηράω except where θηρεύω is required for the metre.

886 f. **θηλύκτονον "Αρη** Weil, θηλύκτονον ἄγος Francken, δαμέντας Pauw, but probably no emendation is needed.

890. **ἐς** M, ἐπ' recc., but *come to* is appropriate.

897 f. **σπόρος** Sikes and Willson, σποράς MSS, perhaps by assimilation to **τῆσδε.** A substantive with θρασύς, **τόξοισι κλεινός** seems indispensable. Wecklein conjectures τόξοισι κλεινὸς <ἶνις> ὃς πόνων [ἐκ τῶνδ'] ἐμέ.

911. **πταίουσ'** M, παίουσ' recc.

913. **ἢ σοφὸς [ἦν] ὅς:** ἦν is omitted by Triclinius: it is often understood in formulae like this.

923. **<πότνιαι>** Winckelmann, metri gratia.

929. **ἀμαλαπτομέναν** Dindorf (Weil γ' ἀμαλ.) for γάμῳ δαπτομέναν MSS. The schol. ἅμα τῷ γάμῳ· λείπει γὰρ τὸ ἅμα may indicate an original gloss τῷ γάμῳ written over ἅμα δαπτομέναν, a mistake for ἀμαλαπτομέναν.

931. ἐμοὶ δέ γ' Hermann, metri gratia, ὅτε Arnold, ἐμοὶ δ' ὅτι MSS.

932. οὐδὲ δέδια Hermann, οὐ δέδια MSS.

933. [ἔρως] rejected by Schuetz.

939. αὐθάδη φρονῶν m¹, recc. : αὐθάδης φρενῶν M, recc., which edd. accept (for the absence of ὤν with καίπερ v. G. 1571), in the sense of αὐθάδης φρένας, quoting Eur. Bacch. 33 παράκοποι φρενῶν : there however the gen. is ablatival.

966. τοῦδ' ἔτ' Elmsley; τοῦδέ γ' MSS (two τοῦδε), 'worse than *that*' (as though death were not a great punishment); but this is not appropriate to the Chorus.

977. ἐφημέροις recc., others τὸν ἐφημέροις : τὸν ἡμέροις M.

980. τ' Elmsley rejects, making γάμους the antecedent of ὧν, cf. 941 ; but this is not necessary.

982. ἔκαστ' ἔκφραζε recc., ἔκαστα φράζε M, recc.

997. κατούρισας Hermann ; καθώρο*σας (read by Sikes and Willson καθώροσας), the o made from ι, M ; καθώρμισας, καθώρισας, καθώρουσας &c. recc. Edd. mostly give καθώρμισας, but this was probably a gloss on the less prosaic κατούρισας and partly written over it in M (ἐπουρίζω is glossed by ἐφορμίζω or ἐφορμέω in Eum. 137, Eur. Andr. 610, Plat. Alcib. II. 147 A, and Hesych. s.vv. ἐπούρισας, ἐπούρισεν : Headlam).

1000 f., assigned to Prometheus in the MSS, were restored to Hermes by Erfurdt.

1006. συμφορᾶς rec., συμφοραῖς M, recc., which edd. retain as a causal dat. like Cho. 80 (81) δακρύω...δεσπόταν τύχαις, *at the misfortunes*: but such a departure from the ordinary gen. with a verb of accusing is unlikely.

1012. ·Lachmann conjectures ΠΡ. ὤμοι. | EP. <ὤμοι·> τόδε Ζεὺς τοὔπος... *That word 'Alas'*.... There is no other case in Aesch. (except Sept. 203 (217), which is doubtful) of an iambic trimeter divided between two speakers.

1018. ὥστε παῖδά με Hermann ; ὡς παῖδά με M : ὡς παῖδ' ὄντα με recc., which should mean *thinking me* or *inasmuch as I am a child*.

1040 f. μαλθάσσῃ λιταῖς | ἐμαῖς MSS, μαλθάσσῃ κέαρ | λιταῖς ἐμαῖς Robortelli, whence Porson and most edd. μαλθάσσῃ κέαρ | λιταῖς.

1063. See expl. n.

1089. μή <οὐ> Wecklein, μή MSS. At 654 and 813 M has μή corrected by m to μὴ οὐ. [However the MSS attest a good many cases of μή with the inf. (mostly when preceded by τό), where μὴ οὐ would be more regular ; and in some, e.g. Soph. O. T. 1387 τὸ μὴ ἀποκλαῦσαι,

Ar. Pax 315 μὴ ἐξελκύσαι, the metre precludes the insertion of οὐ. See M. and T. 809, 812.]

1090. **ἡ τοῦδ' εὐχή** Winckelmann ; ἦ τοῦδ' εὐτυχῇ M, with εἰ τάδ' in margin m¹ ; εἰ τάδ' εὐτυχῇ, εὐτυχεῖ &c. recc. ; ἡ τοῦδ' αὐχή (perhaps right), ἡ τοῦδε τύχη, εἰ τάδ' ἔτ' αὐχεῖ &c., edd.

INDICES TO COMMENTARY.

Arabic numerals refer to the Explanatory Notes by lines (unless otherwise stated), Roman numerals to the Introduction by pages.

I. GREEK.

II. ENGLISH.

For EU product safety concerns, contact us at Calle de José Abascal, 56–1°,
28003 Madrid, Spain or eugpsr@cambridge.org.

www.ingramcontent.com/pod-product-compliance
Ingram Content Group UK Ltd.
Pitfield, Milton Keynes, MK11 3LW, UK
UKHW020313140625
459647UK00018B/1853